Andrea Nastri
Giuliana Vespere

essays by

a Andreini
in Powers
an Woods
Peter Bishop

ON THE ROAD city
London

ON THE ROAD
Editor of collection
Laura Andreini

editorial project
Forma Edizioni srl, Firenze, Italia
redazione@formaedizioni.it
www.formaedizioni.it

editorial direction
Laura Andreini

authors
Andrea Nastri*
Giuliana Vespere**

editorial staff
Maria Giulia Caliri
Livia D'Aliasi

graphic design
Silvia Agozzino
Isabella Peruzzi

translations
Katy Hannan
Karen Whittle

texts by
Laura Andreini
Alan Powers
Brendan Woods
Peter Bishop

* **Andrea Nastri**, architect, PhD in History of Architecture, is a lecturer under contract at the LUM Jean Monnet University. He works for the Naples Municipality, and is involved in restoration of monuments and urban redevelopment. He writes for newspapers and international architectural magazines and has published a series of specialised books on architecture.

** **Giuliana Vespere**, architect, PhD in Architectural and Urban planning, is a lecturer under contract at the LUM Jean Monnet University. She works for the Naples Municipality and has written several books on modern and contemporary architecture.

© 2020 Forma Edizioni srl, Firenze

Second Edition: August 2020

ISBN 978-88-55210-41-6

Table of contents

Guidebook as a tool

On the Road is a collection of contemporary architecture guidebooks whose purpose is to tell about a place, whether a city or larger area, through its architectural works chosen to be visited and experienced directly.

The guidebook has a convenient special jacket that opens into a map marking the location of the architectural works and interesting sites to visit. On the back are miniature images and addresses of the architectural works described in detail within.

The book starts with short essays explaining the city or area's present day and history and outlining possible future scenarios with planned or imminent projects. Each work features a photograph of the whole, an architectural drawing (plan or section), a short description, and facts including architect, type, year of construction, address, website, and how to visit it.

The finest architecture of each city and suggested routes are represented by this collection of not-to-be-missed, "timeless" buildings that uniquely define their settings. General information and useful tips for travelers help them optimize their visits and quickly understand the essence of the place described.

Museums, theatres, restaurants, hotels and a list of top architectural firms working in the city let visitors turn a regular trip into an opportunity for study or work.

Note: The pinpoints outside the maps at the beginning of the itineraries are viewable on the rear of the book jacket.

London

Laura Andreini*

Recent new dynamic urban and architectural changes in London led to the need for a new edition of the guide only three years after its initial publication. It is interesting to note that the new projects added to those in the previous issue are located in five of the six itineraries proposed. This is proof of the homogeneous evolution throughout the city: no area of the metropolis remains frozen in time. On the contrary, most of the city is in a state of constant transformation: restoration of 19th century buildings and redevelopment of urban areas with the addition of new public spaces for the local population and visitors.

In 1999, the Urban Task Force, led by Richard Rogers, began to introduce principles for reorganising public spaces in enclosed form and building densification as well as suburban functional mixing. Without a doubt, these policies have produced very successful urban planning results and continue to be very effective today. I wish to focus attention on the types of projects that have been added to the previous edition. As well as new construction or restoration, more than half of the 11 projects have involved the redevelopment of the surrounding public space. Bloomberg's new London Headquarters presents a new covered public space, as does St James Market and the Coal Drops Yard, where the curving roofs of the two structures unite to form a covered plaza. Angel Court and London Wall Place have included careful design of the surrounding public space, while the Gasholders London apartments were built together with Gasholder Park, a gasometer transformed to create an urban park.

As well as the restoration of historic buildings based on modern composition and design, structurally innovative, and with strong visual impact, urban planning in London maintains a careful focus on development according to principles of high quality construction and sustainability, for good livability standards. In fact, London is the capital of Cycle Superhighways, cycling routes that run from the suburbs to the city centre: an excellent system able to encourage a more appropriate lifestyle and to provide a "slow" opportunity for analysing new urban trends within the city. Once more, the capital of the United Kingdom confirms its role as a fascinating city for contemporary architecture lovers. Thanks to rapid transit by various means of efficient public transport, unconventional but extremely attractive public spaces, and buildings with great architectural impact, visitors to London will feel immersed in an atmosphere of contemporary design, more than in any other place.

* Laura Andreini is architect and associate professor at DIDA, University of Florence. Co-founder of Studio Archea where she still works, she is also writer and deputy editor for *area* magazine.

Political / geographical facts

country
England, United Kingdom

language
english

area code
+ 44 (20)

coordinates
51° 30' 26" N
0° 07' 39" E

area
1,572.15 sq. km

population
8,908,081

density
5,666 inhabitants
/ sq.km

time zone
UTC+0

city website
www.london.gov.uk

Administrative districts

1. City of London
2. City of Westminster
3. Kensington and Chelsea
4. Hammersmith and Fulham
5. Wandsworth
6. Lambeth
7. Southwark
8. Tower Hamlets
9. Hackney
10. Islington
11. Camden
12. Brent
13. Ealing
14. Hounslow
15. Richmond
16. Kingston
17. Merton
18. Sutton
19. Croydon
20. Bromley
21. Lewisham
22. Greenwich
23. Bexley
24. Havering
25. Barking and Dagenham
26. Redbridge
27. Newham
28. Waltham Forest
29. Haringey
30. Enfield
31. Barnet
32. Harrow
33. Hillingdon

General information
useful addresses and numbers

INFORMATION OFFICES

City of London Information Centre
St Paul's Churchyard
London EC4M 8BX
+44 (0)20 7332 1456
Mon - Sat / 9.30 am - 5.30 pm
Sun / 10 am - 4 pm
25 - 26 December / closed

Piccadilly Circus Travel Information Centre
Piccadilly
London W1J 9HS
+44 343 222 1234
Mon - Sun / 9.30 am - 4 pm

EMERGENCY SERVICES

Police, Fire Department and Emergency
medical service: 112 or 999

URBAN TRANSPORT

The site tfl.gov.uk provides useful information on
all means of transport available in the city, how to
buy tickets, and ordinary and season ticket fares*. It
also gives information in real time on delays, works
underway and station closures.

Taxi
One-Number Taxi 0871 871 8710
Dial-A-Cab 020 7253 5000
Radio Taxis 020 7272 0272
Taxis can also be booked online at www.kabbee.com
or using the Hailo App downloadable from App Store
or Google Play: uk.mytaxi.com

Bicycle rentals
Santander Cycles
It costs 2 pounds to access a bike for 24 hours.
The first 30 minutes of every journey are free, then
the service costs £2 every 30 minutes.
For rapid access to the hire service, download the
Santander Cycles App from App Store or Google Play.

Car sharing
There are many web sites and apps for access to car
sharing. tfl.gov.uk/modes/driving/car-clubs

* The cheapest and handiest way of paying for public transport
  in London is the rechargeable Oyster Card, which can be used
  to pay for reduced-price single fares and season tickets on
  the whole transport network.

GENERAL CONSULATE OF FRANCE
21 Cromwell Road, London SW7 2EN
+44 (0)20 7073 1200

GENERAL CONSULATE OF GERMANY
23 Belgrave Square / Chesham Place
London SW1X 8PZ
+44 (0)20 7824 1300

EMBASSY OF ITALY
14 Three Kings Yard, London W1K 4EH
+44 (0)20 7312 2200

EMBASSY OF THE UNITED STATES
24 Grosvenor Square, London W1A 2LQ
+44 (0)20 7499 9000

EMBASSY OF THE PEOPLE'S REPUBLIC OF CHINA
49 Portland Place, London W1B 1JL
+44 (0)20 7631 1430

HOW TO PHONE

From a local landline: Just dial the number, including
the city code (0)20

From a foreign landline: Dial the international code
(+44), city code (20) and number

Useful tips

1. London offers a vast choice of accommodation for all pockets. Among the most attractive options are the Charlotte Street Hotel, the city's first boutique hotel, and the characteristic Church Street Hotel with competitive prices situated in the south-east. The Ritz overlooking Green Park excels among the most luxurious and sophisticated options, while **W London Leicester Square/28**, entirely covered in glass and designed by the firm Jestico + Whiles, can be pointed out among the most modern.
In general, the West End, Kensington, Hyde Park, Notting Hill and West London are the most expensive areas, while in the South Bank there are lots of chain hotels with some of the most beautiful views in the city.

2. In addition to taxis (the famous black cabs), the most practical and quick way to get around the city is the Tube, open from 5.30 am to 12.30 am (7.00 am to 11.30 am on Sundays). The buses are also very popular, offering priceless views of the city, especially from the traditional double-deckers, as well as a night service. Then there is the more recent London Overground, an urban railway service that covers a large part of Greater London and part of Hertfordshire.

3. Another way of getting around the city is by bike, which can be taken on the Circle, District, Hammersmith&City and Metropolitan tube lines (except in the rush hour, Mon-Fri 7.30-9.30 am and 4-7 pm). The best option, used by many tourists, is the Santander Cycles bike-sharing service. It has 570 docking stations in the city where you can pick up and leave the bikes.

4. One of the must-dos has to be to observe London from above. To do so there are various alternatives, such as climbing to the top of Renzo Piano's recently completed **The Shard/41**, on South Bank, or going on the incredibly popular London Eye, a stone's throw from Westminster Bridge, which gives a spectacular 360° view of the city. Another interesting panorama can be seen from the seventh-floor restaurant in the **Tate Modern/38**, from which you can admire the view over **St Paul's Cathedral/01**, the Thames and the **Millennium Bridge/39**.

5. London is deservedly famous for its magnificent museums. In some cases, here you can not only admire the works of art, but also important contemporary extensions and renovations. This is the case of **The British Museum**, with the **Great Court/23** designed by Norman Foster (also author of the **Sackler Galleries** at **Burlington House/26**), the **Victoria and Albert Museum**, with the **Exhibition Road Quarter/57** set out according to AL_A's design, as well as the world-famous Tate Modern by Herzog & de Meuron. Among the museums dedicated to architecture and design are the Museum of Architecture (MoA), founded in 2006, and the **London Design Museum/55**, which recently moved to new premises designed by John Pawson.

6. Every year, the London Festival of Architecture takes place in the month of June, celebrating the British capital's architecture with exhibitions, debates, conferences and guided tours. Instead in September visitors can enjoy special free entry to over 700 buildings and private residences organized by the Open House London association. In the past, the event has involved various famous buildings, amongst which **The Gherkin/11**, **City Hall/42**, **Lloyd's of London/09**, the Royal Courts of Justice and the BT Tower.

7. London's parks are ideal for a bit of relaxation, but they also host sports events, open-air theatres, concerts and children's playgrounds. The oldest royal parks (Kensington Gardens, Hyde Park, Green Park, St James's Park and **Regent's Park/63**) were originally large open spaces that the royals used as hunting reserves. Today the city hosts a vast quantity and variety of green areas, from the most well-tended (such as Holland Park and St James's Park) to the most untamed (such as Richmond Park, Finsbury Park and Bushy Park).

8. London's markets sell absolutely everything. Among the biggest are Spitalfields, in the East End, and Camden, in north London. Very famous ones are Covent Garden, an architectural masterpiece and London icon, and Portobello Road, where you can mainly find knickknacks and antiques. Old Spitalfields Market is a very popular indoor market that stretches as far as Brick Lane, where the historic and popular vintage and second-hand market takes place on Sundays. The biggest indoor market in London is Alfies Antique Market where you can find 20th-century designer objects. Finally, there's London's foodie paradise, Borough Market, ideal both for shopping (there's a large variety of fresh products, from fruits and vegetables to cheese and meat) and for a tasty lunch.

9. You can't say you've captured the spirit of London without spending at least one evening in one of its pubs. As is well-known, pub culture is an integral part of the English lifestyle and, especially if you avoid the more commercial ones, you can meet the locals relaxing there after work. For a while now, so-called gastropubs have gained in popularity. Instead of the traditional pubs where you could only drink, at most with a snack, they offer a selection of classic English dishes which fittingly go well with a beer or two.

London: the beauty of chaos

Alan Powers*

If you had to choose a city to demonstrate Chaos Theory in action, London would make a good example. The grid plan of the Roman walled city has long been overlaid by a network of tighter mediaeval streets, presenting obstacles to movement then and blockages caused by historic patterns of land ownership even today. Monarchs lacked the power or money to intervene and as lost ducal palaces stretched along the curve of the Thames towards the seat of government in Westminster, the hinterland filled up with varied forms of building. In 1630, the Earl of Bedford paid £2,000 to King Charles I for permission to develop his land north of the Strand. Inigo Jones, the royal architect, had been to Italy, and brought back the Renaissance, albeit 200 years late. Jones laid out a generous 'piazza' flanked by regular house fronts raised on arcades on two sides. The long axis was closed by the Tuscan portico of a pagan-looking church, a grand gesture still legible today. After the Great Fire of 1666, proposals for a rational street plan were rejected but Inigo's baroque successors, Sir Christopher Wren and Nicholas Hawksmoor, brought an English Baroque style to maturity as they rebuilt St Paul's and the City churches.

Districts became classified by occupation: money and trading in the City, manufacture to the east and north. Lawyers remain in their leafy, traffic-free 'Inns of Court', resembling Oxford or Cambridge colleges, tucked between Westminster and the City. South of the river, docks and warehouses shut off the riverside from the growing population of clerks who walked to work over the few bridges or from Islington in the north. Artists worked in Soho; writers close to the presses of Fleet Street. The aristocratic Estates of the West End of London were composed of standardised elements: terraces like palaces facing the squares with mews behind for horses; cheaper streets, plus shops and markets lurked behind, plus a sprinkling of stone church spires, after the model of Wren, as guarantors of respectability. Each Estate was laid out to create a self-contained miniature universe and even today, pedestrians will find curious obstacles in the street network, where estates reinforce their boundaries rather than making them porous. If Chaos Theory applies to this situation, it shows how living systems adapt to random conditions. A few of the rich and powerful had individually designed town palaces – Spencer House overlooking the Green Park is one survivor – but the terrace house was a model that could be scaled to suit the richest and the poorest alike. Apartment living was almost unknown, although the individual narrow houses were often subdivided and occupied by many households as they fell down the social scale.

Before 1800, 20 minutes' walk would bring you to open country where the edge of the city merged into farms, cottages and villas. Then, fuelled by the demand of an expanding population plus investment money looking for a profitable venture, London mushroomed. Regent Street was a bold speculation under royal patronage, trimming the edge of Soho for a triumphal route for the monarch-in-waiting (later George IV) to ride to Regent's Park. The architect John Nash took urban forms from Bath – the Circus and the Crescent, adding fake palaces gaudily decked in painted plaster over brickwork.

The 'Great Wen', as the radical writer William Cobbett called London, seemed increasingly out of control, its population expanding sixfold in the course of the nineteenth century. Pressure mounted during Queen Victoria's reign as the primitive infrastructure failed to cope. A police force, proper drains, plus institutions of learning including museums and galleries, hospitals and facilities for newly popular sports gave relief, leaving their mark with earnest highly decorated buildings of red brick, often Gothic or Northern European in style. Coal smoke filled the sky from thousands of domestic chimneys and from the locomotives bringing goods and passengers to and from the capital.

After 1880, rising fear of revolution pushed governments into action. London acquired a County Council to control the chaos, taking charge of infrastructure, education and leisure and building social housing as London slums began to be cleared – an operation unfinished even by 1960. London Transport coordinated the operation and the visual style of buses, trams and underground trains, along whose radiating lines grew another ring of suburbs in a triumph of free enterprise housing.

The Second World War left parts of London flattened by bombs. The moment of Modernism had arrived, and architects demanded slabs and towers among green spaces. With ambitious schemes left unfinished as money ran out and ideas changed, this anti-urban approach simply joined the existing chaos. Commercial interests meanwhile caused the second and third great rebuilding of the commercial heart of the City, heedless of heritage until bombs and socialism induced the protection of historic buildings in 1947.

For fifty years after 1931, the total population of London shrank while high-rise housing and offices filled the skyline. Urban motorway projects stalled. Rather than becoming an American city of long commutes and inner ring decay, London learned the lesson of Jane Jacobs that cities live through complexity, becoming by 2000 a people-centred European city for walking, outdoor eating and drinking, an outcome foreshadowed by the City of London's Barbican development, built with the design rigour of a top-quality Georgian urban quarter and standing as a rebuke to the flashy absentee-investor residential towers of recent years that signal a whole new kind of chaos.

* Alan Powers is writer, curator, conservationist and teacher at the London School of Architecture and at the New York University, London.

London post Thatcher

Brendan Woods*

The governance of post-Second World War London has seen a number of changes with the LCC – the London County Council – being replaced by the GLC – the Greater London Council – and the subsequent adoption of a mayoral system introduced in the late 1990s after a period of 'direct rule' following the abolition of the GLC in 1985 by Mrs Thatcher, the Conservative Prime Minister. The result of her dictatorial intervention in the administration of London was Canary Wharf – an offshoot of the City of London, a classic example of urban planning inspired by Laissez-Faire Capitalism along with largely piecemeal commercial development throughout London. However, the development of the Shad Thames area did produce an urbane mixed-use quartier of refurbished warehouses, the Design Museum and Tower Bridge Piazza by Wickham and Associates with its two squares and a new narrow street linking the interior of this urban block. This was followed by a long period of 'bust' as is characteristic.

During this time, the beautiful Sackler Galleries at the Royal Academy by Foster + Partners were completed. A project which owes a lot to Kahn's Kimbell Art Museum and to Italian architecture from the 1950s e.g. Albini and Helg. To my mind one of their most architectural projects and almost good enough to be Italian. This period also saw them complete the Great Court in the British Museum in 2000, which is not so impressive for all its size. Alas it is a very interesting and clever roof on top of a bland refacing of the Reading Room, with crass use of French limestone on the opposing façade rather than the intended Portland stone and it is in effect really a shopping precinct in the heart of this most prestigious of museums. If only James Stirling had been given the commission. There is also the new City Hall down near Tower Bridge which is affectionately known as the Gonad – for obvious reasons – and which few people can take seriously as a public building. The 'public' space adjacent to it is in fact private i.e. no demonstrations may occur there, a strange condition for a public building.

Perhaps inspired by the example of the Guggenheim Bilbao, the London Eye – a giant Ferris wheel sited further up the river – was financed by British Airways (designed by Marks and Barfield) to become a major tourist attraction. An extraordinary piece of engineering, it continues the perception of the South Bank dating from the 1951 Festival of Britain as not really being a serious part of the City. A perception encouraged by the old offices of the GLC – County Hall – being turned into an aquarium.

Ken Livingstone, who had been head of the GLC before it was abolished, was elected Mayor in May 2000 and set about trying to recover some of the policies popular before 1985 e.g. building 'Social Housing' for rent but this was largely frustrated by the neo-liberal policies of New Labour under Tony Blair and Gordon Brown. Various boroughs in central London including Camden and Islington which had produced exceptionally good social housing e.g. Alexandra Road and New River End respectively found it increasingly difficult to build social housing, which was now obliged to be called Affordable Housing – the rents being capped at a percentage of the market rate. However, this has increasingly become Non-Affordable Housing for teachers and service workers, and now we are approaching a situation where under Boris Johnson – the last Mayor from 2008-2016 and a Tory – virtually no Affordable Housing was built in central London resulting in an increasing housing crisis. This is as a direct result of government policies where the private housing market has been allowed to 'let rip' with foreign buyers taking 70% of all new flats/houses, (London is now considered by many to be a major Money Laundering Capital). Sadiq Khan of Labour, the new Mayor, is determined to correct this but has a real battle on his hands.

Ken Livingstone's policies included establishing a Congestion Zone in Central London which, allied with investment in buses, brought about a dramatic change in air quality and ease of movement. He also set in motion the Bike Rental system which subsequently and erroneously became known as Boris Bikes. His contribution to the skyline of London was The Shard by Renzo Piano, signalling the possible expansion of the financial City to the south bank of the river Thames – a truly momentous change. This was made possible by his strategic policy of allowing large-scale redevelopment of certain 'Node' points in central London allied to public transport. The Shard allied to London Bridge Station and Central St Giles, again by Renzo Piano, allied to Tottenham Court Road Station with the new CrossRail transport system currently being built under Oxford Street and which will eventually link Maidenhead and Heathrow to Essex with 200-metre-long trains arriving every 2.5 minutes. Via upgrading of the transport systems and the introduction of bike lanes in inner London the experience of living in and moving about inner London has been transformed. The 2012 Olympics provided the opportunity to redefine and develop the area around Stratford resulting in 'iconic' buildings such as the Aquatics Centre by Zaha Hadid, the monstrous Arcelor Mittal Orbit bauble by Anish Kapoor and Cecil Balmond and a new park bringing a taste of North American landscape design to an area that had been previously quintessentially East London: the joys of modernisation.

The Olympic village produced a novel collection of residential buildings including a witty reference to Classical Greece in the precast panels of the apartment building by Niall McLoughin Architects. Meanwhile in the City, Foster's Gherkin attempted to steal the limelight from Richard Rogers' extraordinary essay in Constructivist office-building from the early 1980s – Lloyd's of London. But it in turn is now somewhat hidden by Rogers Stirk Harbour's latest contribution to futuristic high rise: the so-called Cheesegrater, where an attempt has also been made to create a public space under the building at street level – yet to be successfully resolved. The elegant form and sophisticated construction of this building contrasting with the truly awful 'Walkie Talkie' by Rafael Viñoly which threatens a neighbouring area of the City with its bulbous vulgar profile. The desperate search for novel form to express the brutal reality of rental values – it gets bigger as it goes up resulting in a terrible blight to the views up and down the river. What would Sir Christopher Wren make of it all? And St Paul's fairly recently joined by the dirty brown 'stealth' development by Jean Nouvel to the east adding insult to the injury of the Prince of Wales-inspired reactionary concoction of buildings to the North.

Along with the Livingstone policy of densification of Node Points was the overhaul of the major stations – Brunel's beautiful shed and hotel at Paddington by Grimshaw and Partners (whose terminal for Eurostar at Waterloo now languishes like a disused film set), St Pancras International taking over as the destination and start of European rail journeys with a bravura transformation of the Midland Hotel into a top-class establishment, the concourse transformed into a stunning two-level interchange linking to a new set of platforms serving the Midlands and Kent via HS1 which shares a long stretch of track with Eurostar. This development was also linked with the Olympic site as HS1 delivered spectators from central London to the Olympic site at Stratford in a few minutes. Alongside St Pancras there is also now the Crick Institute, a multimillion science facility run by Sir Paul Nurse, a Nobel Prize winner. This rather rhetorical and melodramatic building opens in early 2017.

Adjacent to St Pancras International and linking to it as a major transport interchange is King's Cross station (trains to and from Cambridge and the University). The entrance to King's Cross was previously experienced via fairly utilitarian structures obscuring its 'heroic' façade. These have been demolished and an operatic semicircular ticket hall with shops added to the left-hand side. This results in the original entrance façade becoming the exit. Perverse architecturally (and historically) but possibly the only solution given the much increased number of passengers now using the station. It serves as a pivot to St Pancras and the area to the north.

The surrounding area had seen itself sink into a miserable and rather sordid state through the 70s and 80s – due to drug pedalling and prostitution – and is now in the process of being transformed into a new 'quartier' by a developer called Argent with an avenue of 'interesting' office buildings by well-known architects – Chipperfield, Eric Parry and Allies and Morrison inter alia – leading to the relocated Central St Martins School of Art in the old Granary Building north of King's Cross Station on the other side of the Regent's Canal. Aficionados of the Boulting Brothers and the charming English films of the early 1950s will now be hard pushed to recognise the site of the house from the *Ladykillers*. That area has now seen the redevelopment of York Way into a residential highway with Kings' Place by Dixon Jones signalling a starting point.

Argent's attempts at creating a new urban quarter eschew traditional European models or indeed our own Georgian model of streets and squares for a more North American model – without the cars – sadly allowing larger areas of inner London to become private (and therefore denying the users their rights as citizens) with private security guards. Google occupy one of the buildings overlooking a wedge-shaped square with Parry's latest homage to twentieth-century Chicago at its head.

However, an exemplary piece of urbanism has recently been achieved in the new addition to Tate Modern where Herzog & de Meuron with their twisting brick-clad tower have achieved a consummate resolution of adding to the formidable bulk of the original power station, creating an extraordinary new series of galleries and support spaces while finding urban sense in the ad hoc arrangement of the surrounding streets and office blocks. This 'tour de force' is exemplary in demonstrating the skills of architects who ingested urbanism with their mother's milk. They were taught by Aldo Rossi, as it happens. OMA's recent building for the Rothchild's behind St Stephen Walbrook is another exemplar of a European sensibility, mixing urbanistic sleight of hand with witty sophistication. Its morphological inflexions to St Stephen's revelling in the complexity of the site. We all hope that London will not suffer too greatly from the results of Brexit.

London has become one of the most culturally diverse cities in the world. Let's hope it builds on this by nurturing its native genius and importing the best ideas from the rest of the world rather than succumb to the suburbanising ideas of North America and its corporate culture.

* Brendan Woods AA Dipl RIBA is a practising architect who has taught in a number of architectural schools including the AA, Cambridge, Bath, Bartlett and Glasgow.

London the Resilient City

Peter Bishop*

Throughout its history London has been a mercantile city, dominated by commerce and trade. Its fortunes have fluctuated, but London has been resilient enough to cope with changes in trade patterns, plague, war, the creation and loss of empire and more recently the emergence of a globalised economy. London's commercial power has always granted it a degree of independence from centralised government and this tension is one of the defining themes of English history. London's good fortune is that no ruler has ever had the power to superimpose grand plans on the city. Growth has been largely through private capital raised on private estates. The city as a result appears to be largely organic, but there are underlying structures, conventions rather than plans.

By the mid fourteenth century prolonged peace (that did not prevail in Europe until the early nineteenth century) allowed London to abandon its city walls and spread outwards. It was outside the old city limits that the informal city began; slums, waste tips, fair and pleasure grounds, slaughterhouses, stews, gardens and markets. From the seventeenth century onwards London's growth was planned through a series of great land speculations. The 'Great Estates' laid out on a series of small-scale, off-set orthogonal grids resulted in Mayfair, Marylebone, Bloomsbury and Belgravia. Still largely in single ownership they represent some of the most successful examples of urban planning (and financial return) anywhere in the world. The Georgian terrace and square represent one of the most enduring architectural typologies in the London vernacular.

Around the middle of the seventeenth century expanding British trade and overseas territories consolidated London's position as one of the most important mercantile centres in the world. With trade came banking, insurance and venture capital companies. London expanded and districts became classified by occupation: money and trading in the City, docks and warehouses in the east and manufacturing to the east and north. The districts south of the river, previously pleasure gardens, became centres for trade and commerce and this pattern still underlies the character of these areas today. These are compact areas with a fine urban grain accommodating diverse industries and populations, often with the rich and poor living side by side in close proximity.

As London expanded it began the process of absorbing existing settlements on its periphery. Villages were annexed into the growing city, but still retained their individual character and became the early suburbs. Islington, Hampstead, Highgate and Chelsea, for example, still retain their individual character today making London a 'city of villages'. The Victorian age brought prosperity and mechanical invention. The railways transformed travel and allowed the city to expand rapidly. They acted as arteries to fuel the growth of the city, carrying building materials, coal, food and iron and steel in quantities hitherto undreamed of. They literally built the city, fed it and with the construction of the first underground railway system, carried people around it. Growth, however, brought its own problems. London had minimal drainage and poor water supply and this brought cholera and other epidemics. A new sewerage system was built (and is still in use today), a police force established, gas and electricity introduced. A whole civic infrastructure was established including museums and galleries, schools and universities, hospitals and of course the metropolitan park. London decentralised and suburbanised. Metroland, the low density, garden suburb appeared as London devoured the open country, and annexed the villages around it. The eventual backlash came with the designation of a Green Belt around London, constraining its outward growth just before the outbreak of the Second World War.

The heavy bombing that London endured during the Second World War has had a significant impact on the city today. Much of central and east London was destroyed as the bombing punched holes in the fabric of the city. Although the destruction was immense, it created the conditions for the replanning of London and the clearance of poor quality slum housing. Critically it allowed the rehousing of much of the population within in the same neighbourhoods, perpetuating the fine social grain of the city. Experiments with Modernist housing were surprisingly limited to a number of infill estates and high-rise blocks.

Attempts to solve transportation through the construction of urban motorways were soon abandoned due to public opposition. London flirted briefly with the notion of large-scale rationalist planning but quickly rejected it. It was never the London style. The growth of the conservation movement in the late 1960s put an end to Modernist solutions and has preserved much of the historic fabric that defines the city today.

But there was another aspect of London's growth that is key to understanding the city today – the immigrant. London grew as a city of opportunity where one could achieve unimagined wealth. It attracted the ambitious, the curious and the outcast from the countryside and from overseas. These included traders from the Baltic, merchants from Holland and refugees from religious persecution from France. London was cosmopolitan, it was tolerant, it was politically stable and it was a place to make money, attributes that endure today.

The decline in London's post-war population reversed at the end of the 1980s as Britain went through the major social and economic upheavals of the Thatcher era. The City was deregulated and a new spirit of unfettered market-driven capitalism saw the regeneration of the old dock areas and the construction of Canary Wharf, London's second central business district. London started to attract footloose capital and talent from around the world. From 2000, with the re-establishment of devolved London government, a dynamic, fast-growing and cosmopolitan population and emerging new 'creative' industries, London has emerged into the global city, showcased by the 2012 London Olympics.

Today London stands at a crossroads. Faced with the challenges of rapid growth and speculative development based on overseas investment in property as a tradable commodity, London faces the risk of forcing out the key workers and creative industries that are the mainstay of its economy. Brexit and London's global position are still unresolved and there are renewed uncertainties about the future. But London is diverse, resilient and adaptable. London is a city that constantly reinvents itself.

* Peter Bishop is professor of Urban Design at The Bartlett School of Architecture, University College London and a distinguished visiting scholar at the University of Technology Sydney. He is also a director at the London-based architects' practice Allies and Morrison.

London Bridge
Tower (The Shard)

Guy's Hospital Tower

The News Building

Southwark Cathedral

St Paul's Cathedral

125 London Wall

One New Change

City of London School

Millennium Bridge

© Mauro Simpadisa

Angel Court

One New Change

Tower 42

The Leadenhall Building
(The Cheesegrater)

20 Fenchurch Street
(The Walkie Talkie)

The Willis Building

Lloyd's of London

Twenty Gracechurch Street

Rothschild Bank
London Headquarters

Bloomberg's New
London Headquarters

©Paolo Novello / Alamy Foto Stock

Strategies for visiting London

A lifetime wouldn't be long enough to really visit such a vast and historical city as London, but to get quite a good idea ten or so days could suffice, perhaps with the resolution to return as soon as possible. Owing to the number and importance of the works of architecture proposed and the possibility of visiting the interior of each of them, each tour requires at least a couple of days, except Tour E, for which one day is enough.

Tour A | The City
The tour passes through the beating heart of the city, that is, the financial centre and immediate surroundings; an area where no more than 10,000 people live, but at least 330.000 work. Of the historic buildings, the must-sees are **St Paul's Cathedral/01** and the Tower of London. A walk through this densely packed district will enable you to admire some of its famous buildings close-up, from the more 'dated' ones, such as the **Lloyd's of London/09** building, to the more recent ones, such as **30 St Mary Axe (The Gherkin)/11**, the **Heron Tower/12** and **The Leadenhall Building (The Cheesegrater)/10**.

Tour B | Westminster - West End
The area to the west of the City hosts some of the most important museums in the world, such as **The British Museum/23** and the National Gallery, but also the smaller but equally as interesting Soane Museum, **Somerset House/21**, **Burlington House/26** and **Banqueting House/29**, as well as **Westminster Abbey/31** and much more besides. The area of Westminster, and more precisely Westminster Borough, is also the political centre of the whole of England. Here, in the radius of just a few hundred metres, we find Buckingham Palace and the Palace of Westminster, with the new **Portcullis House/30**. Even though it is an ancient and consolidated part of the city, in recent years the area has been vastly regenerated, for example in the **Central St Giles Court Development/24** by Renzo Piano.

Tour C | South Bank - Greenwich - South London
The tour includes all the buildings to the south of the Thames. The part alongside the city centre, South Bank, is an area that has undergone a great renewal and regeneration process in recent years. Once neglected, today it has many attractions: from the panoramic London Eye to the **Tate Modern/38**, connected to the City by the **Millennium Bridge/39**, from the highly popular Borough Market to the new skyscraper, **The Shard/41**. The Greenwich area is famous above all for Greenwich Park and its **Royal Observatory/45**, passed through by the meridian line. Also not to be missed are the **Old Royal Naval College/43**, Cutty Sark, National Maritime Museum and Greenwich Peninsula with its contemporary buildings. Two trips further south can take you to visit the **Evelyn Grace Academy/49**, in Brixton, and **Burntwood School/52** in Earlsfield.

Tour D | Kensington - Hyde Park - West London

The main feature of the Kensington district is its greenness, with Hyde Park and the adjacent Kensington Gardens, as well as its three incredibly important museums, the Natural History Museum, Science Museum and the **Victoria and Albert Museum**, whose **Exhibition Road Quarter/57** was inaugurated during 2017. Also worth pointing out are the **London Design Museum/55** in Holland Park, and the surrounding area revamped by West 8 and OMA. Every year the Serpentine Galleries create a new Serpentine Pavilion in the Kensington Gardens, designed by the most important architects in the world (the 2020 pavilion is by Counterspace), with Zaha Hadid the name behind the restoration and extension of the **Serpentine Sackler Gallery/59**.

Tour E | Regent's Park - North London

Regent's Park and the curved **Regent Street/63** which links it to St James's Park and the city centre came into being around 1820, their designer, the ingenious John Nash, inspired by Bath's eighteenth-century Neoclassical buildings. The tour then passes through Camden. Regent's Canal, close to the world-famous Camden Market, is the site of the **Grand Union Canal Walk Housing/64** and King's Cross. A disreputable area until the end of the last century, now it is completely transformed, also thanks to the realization of the British Library and the regeneration of **King's Cross/66** and St Pancras. A deviation north will take you to the **London Metropolitan University Graduate Centre/69**, the first project realized by Daniel Libeskind in London.

Tour F | Docklands - Olympic Park - East End

Unlike the area to the west of London's historic core, the area to the east has remained generally poorer. It is quite chaotic and multi-ethnic still today. Since the London Overground opened, it has become easier to visit this area, which is not well served by the Tube. Today the Docklands, the largest dockland area in the world until the 1960s, is full of skyscrapers hosting financial offices, most remarkably the **One Canada Square (Canary Wharf Tower)/78** by Cesar Pelli.

The Emirates Air Line, the first urban cable car ever built in the United Kingdom, links the Royal Docks, and the **Excel Exhibition Centre/82**, to the Greenwich peninsula on the other side of the Thames.

The realization of the Olympic Park for the 2012 Olympic Games was an occasion to regenerate the whole area, from Hackney to Stratford, starting with the reclamation of the River Lee and the adjacent land. The Olympic Stadium is also worth a visit in addition to the buildings described in the guide, such as the **Aquatics Centre/74** and the **Velodrome/75**.

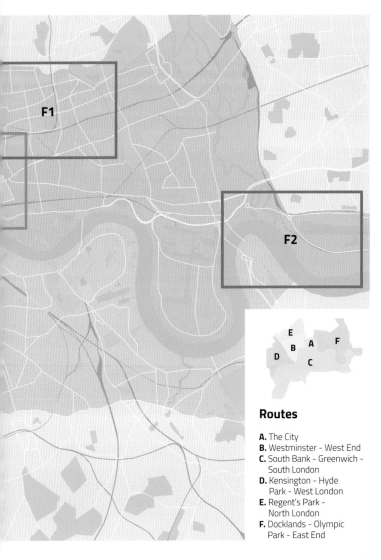

F1

F2

E
B A
F
D B
C

Routes

A. The City
B. Westminster - West End
C. South Bank - Greenwich -
South London
D. Kensington - Hyde
Park - West London
E. Regent's Park -
North London
F. Docklands - Olympic
Park - East End

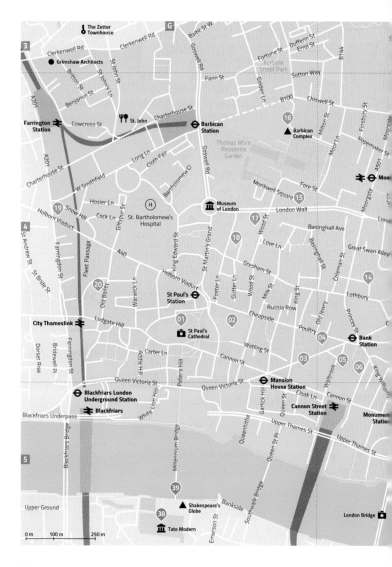

The Zetter Townhouse

Clerkenwell Rd

Clerkenwell Rd

Baltic St W

G

Fortune St

Dufferin St

Errol St

B144

● Grimshaw Architects

St John's St

Goswell Rd

Fortune Street Park

Sutton Way

Britton St

St John's La

Fann St

Golden Ln

B100

Chiswell St

Milton St

Finsbury St

Benjamin St

A201

Charterhouse St

16 ▲ Barbican Complex

Moor Ln

Ropemaker St

Cowcross St

Cloth Fair

St. John

Barbican Station

Thomas More Residents Garden

Fore St

≢ Moo

Farrington Station

Charterhouse St

Long Ln

Goswell Rd

Monkwell Square

15

London Wall

Moorgate

A201

W Smithfield

Hosier Ln

Bartholomew Cl

Museum of London

A501

Lond

Charterhouse St

Snow Hill

Cock Ln

Giltspur St

St. Bartholomew's Hospital

H

17

Wood St

Basinghall Ave

Great Swan Alley

19

Holborn Viaduct

A4

A40

King Edward St

St Martin's Grand

18

Love Ln

Gresham St

Coleman St

Basinghall St

14

Lothbury

4

St Andrew St

Farringdon St

Fleet Passage

Warwick Ln

Old Bailey

Holborn Viaduct

Foster St

Gutter Ln

Wood St

Milk St

King St

Russia Row

Cheapside

Poultry

Old Jewry

Princes St

St Bride St

20

Ludgate Hill

St Paul's Station

01 St Paul's Cathedral

02

04

Bank Station

City Thameslink

Carter Ln

Watling St

03

05

06

King Williams

Bridewell Pl

Addle Hill

Peter's Hill

Cannon St

Mansion House Station

Wallbrook

Cannon St

Dorset Rise

Queen Victoria St

Queen Victoria St

Garlick Hill

Queen's St

Cloak Ln

Cannon Street Station

Monument Statio

Blackfriars London Underground Station

White Lion Hill

Blackfriars

Queenhithe

Upper Thames St

Upper Thames St

Blackfriars Underpass

5

Millennium Bridge

Blackfriars Bridge

Bankside

Southwark Bridge

Queen St Pl

Upper Ground

39

38 🏛 Tate Modern

▲ Shakespeare's Globe

Emerson St

London Bridge

0 m   100 m   250 m

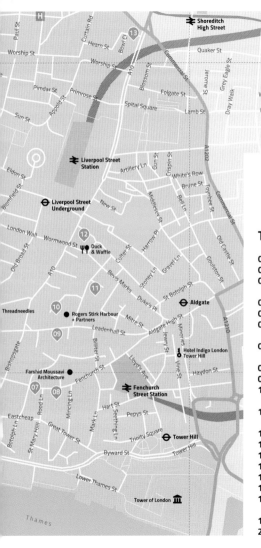

The City

01. St Paul's Cathedral
02. One New Change
03. Bloomberg's New
    London Headquarters
04. Number One Poultry
05. St Stephen Walbrook
06. Rothschild Bank
    London Headquarters
07. 20 Fenchurch Street
    (The Walkie Talkie)
08. Plantation Place
09. Lloyd's of London
10. The Leadenhall Building
    (The Cheesegrater)
11. 30 St Mary Axe
    (The Gherkin)
12. Heron Tower
13. Principal Tower
14. Angel Court
15. London Wall Place
16. The Barbican Complex
17. 88 Wood Street
18. Lloyds Banking Group
    Headquarters
19. Sixty London
20. New Ludgate

01. St Paul's Cathedral

St Paul's Churchyard
London EC4M 8AD

Mon - Thu / 8.30 am - 6 pm
Fri / 8.30 am - 5 pm

+44 (0) 20 72468350
reception@stpaulscathedral.
org.uk
www.stpauls.co.uk

 Central
St Paul's

Among the most iconic buildings in London, St Paul's Cathedral, designed by Sir Christopher Wren and completed in 1711, is one of the most famous examples of English Baroque.

Despite its enormous size, the cathedral is outstanding for its compositional harmony. The front façade features two side towers framing a classical Greek temple portico composed of two orders of paired columns. The interior is remarkable for its majestic sobriety; the presbytery is decorated with beautiful gilded Byzantine mosaics, while the crypt holds the tombs of great historical figures such as Lord Nelson, the Duke of Wellington, Winston Churchill, and Christopher Wren himself.

The famous dome is set on a double drum surrounded by columns; it is 108 metres tall and is the highest in London, offering magnificent views of the city.

In 2007, the City of London Information Centre, designed by Make Architects, was built opposite the south transept of the cathedral. It is a dynamic structure with strong visual impact whose modern shape integrates harmoniously within this context of great historical, architectural, and urban significance.

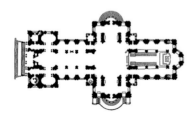

architects
Christopher Wren

type
church

construction
1708

02. One New Change

1 New Change
London EC4M 9AF

Mon - Fri / 10 am - 7 pm
Sat / 10 am - 6 pm
Sun / 12 am - 6 pm

+44 (0) 20 70028900
enquiries@
onenewchange.com
www.onenewchange.com

Central
St Paul's

The building, Jean Nouvel's first work in Great Britain, is situated right in the heart of the City, just a stone's throw from St Paul's Cathedral and Cheapside. The building's unusual layout derives from the delicate relationship with the context and the church, its long central pedestrian passageway an axis creating a perspective towards St Paul's.

One New Change has a many-sided, irregular shape, and is clad by 6,300 reflective glass panels of different degrees of opacity, with 22 shades of brown and over 250 print patterns. Contrary to this linear and matt exterior, the interior has a sculpted and polished feel.

The building hosts 60 shops and restaurants on the first three floors, offices on the upper floors and what can be described as an urban square on the top, with green areas, coffee shops and a restaurant affording a beautiful view over the cathedral and the city.

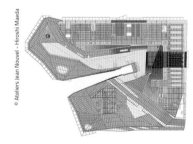

© Ateliers Jean Nouvel - Hiroshi Maeda

© Marco Mugnai

architects
Ateliers Jean Nouvel

type
retail, offices

construction
2010

03. Bloomberg's New London Headquarters

3 Queen Victoria Street
London EC4N 4TQ

external viewing only

www.bloomberg.com/london

**Central / Northern /
Waterloo & City**
Bank

The project for the new European headquarters of the famous American financial software and media company was the result of a synergy between the architects and the owner, Mike Bloomberg, who stated from the beginning that he wanted the design to focus on better working conditions for employees. The complex is composed of two buildings united by bridges over an arcade that forms a new covered public space in the heart of the City, close to the Church of St Stephen Walbrook. The façades are composed of a sandstone structural frame enclosing floor to ceiling glass windows in various widths, with scores of flexible large-scale bronze fins in different formats that are orientated for internal shade and ventilation. The entrance lobby leads to a very dramatic open space that the architects have called "Vortex"; a double-height space created by the union of three large, inclined, curving timber shells. Another striking element is the complex hypotrochoid looped ramp that flows through the full height of the building. The ceilings are constructed completely from polished aluminium panels that incorporate lighting, cooling elements and acoustic damping in an integrated energy-saving system.

© Foster + Partners

© Nigel Young / Foster + Partners

architects
Foster + Partners

type
offices

construction
2017

04. Number One Poultry

1 Poultry
London EC2R 8JR

partly open to the public

 Central / Northern / Waterloo & City
Bank

The office and retail building is situated on the corner between Poultry and Queen Victoria Street. The site was previously host to a listed building designed in 1870 by John Belcher, and a few years before had also been earmarked for an office tower by Mies van der Rohe.

The building comprises various juxtaposed volumes, with façades clad in horizontal stripes of pink and yellow limestone. Like all Postmodern buildings, it contains a wealth of more or less sophisticated symbolic references; for example, it features a tower on the corner façade that is often associated with a submarine control tower and a large lock-shaped opening.

When it was completed, no less than 20 years after the first project draft (and five years after Stirling's death), the success of Postmodernism had already very much peaked; this may also explain the cool welcome given to the building by a large part of the public and critics.

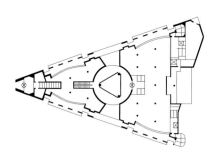

architects
James Stirling and Associates

type
retail, offices

construction
1998

05. St Stephen Walbrook

39 Walbrook
London EC4N 8BN

open to the public

+44 (0) 20 76269000
@ststephenwalbrook.net
ststephenwalbrook.net/

**Central / Northern /
Waterloo & City**
Bank

Wedged between Mansion House and a modern office block, St Stephen Walbrook is situated on the site of the old church of the same name, dating from the 15th century and destroyed in the Great Fire of London in 1666. It was built following the design of Christopher Wren in 1679, in many ways acting as a prototype for his subsequent St Paul's Cathedral.
The church, a masterpiece of English Baroque, has a symmetrical floor plan and counts 16 pillars with Corinthian capitals which support richly ornate architraves. In turn, these hold up a large semispherical dome with stucco decorations. Standing out on the exterior are the tall bell tower with pyramidal steeple, and the dome with its copper covering. Inside, among other things, the church hosts a fine baptism font and a travertine altar made in 1972 by the famous British sculptor Henry Moore.

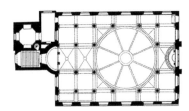

© David Iliff

architects
Christopher Wren

type
church

construction
1680

06. Rothschild Bank London Headquarters

New Court, St Swithin's Lane
London EC4N 8AL

external viewing only

+44 (0) 20 72805000

**Central / Northern /
Waterloo & City**
Bank

Rothschild Bank first set up its headquarters here in the New Court area in 1865. The new OMA building, the latest regeneration of the original Victorian edifice, is raised above street level in order to link St Swithin's Lane, a narrow mediaeval alleyway, back up to the church of St Stephen Walbrook. This way the new building at least in part recreates the old spatial relations in this densely built-up area of the city.

The building is the combination of a cube and four simple adjacent volumes. The façade is made of structural steel, clad with dark glass. At the top, above a roof garden, another suspended three-floor cube – the "Sky Pavilion" – stands out against the skyline, apparently wishing to echo the vertical form of the nearby St Stephen Walbrook church tower. This structure hosts the meeting rooms and a multi-purpose space affording an extraordinary and unusual view over the city.

architects
OMA

type
offices

construction
2011

07. 20 Fenchurch Street (The Walkie Talkie)

20 Fenchurch Street
London EC3M 3BY

partly open to the public

www.20fenchurchstreet.co.uk

Circle / District
Monument

This controversial 37-floor building, situated in the heart of the capital's square mile, was given the nickname of "Walkie Talkie Building" owing to its very unusual shape. The building soars softly and smoothly up to its 177-metre summit, enveloped in glass casing and vertical solar screens along the east and west which extend up to the roof. The lower level floors are smaller, in adaptation to the lack of space and density of the historic urban context of the City, while the higher floors are larger, offering more space for offices, gardens and eating areas, as well as marvellous views over London as far as the eye can see.

20 Fenchurch Street is used for tertiary and commercial purposes, and is rounded off by a spectacular sky garden on the three top floors. A latest-generation skyscraper in terms of sustainability, it incorporates many advanced solutions, such as the use of photovoltaic panels and the reuse of waste water.

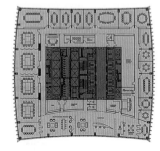

architects
Rafael Viñoly Architects

type
retail, offices

construction
2014

08. Plantation Place

30 Fenchurch Street
London EC3M 3BE

partly open to the public

www.plantationplaceec3.com

Circle / District
Monument

The complex, which is one of the largest interventions made in recent decades in the heart of the City, consists of two buildings. The main one, built along Fenchurch Street, is set out over three basement levels and 15 floors above ground, while the second, known as Plantation Place South, is 10 floors high. The buildings are made up of juxtaposed regular glazed volumes, which become lighter the further up you go. The façades are ventilated and have screens to regulate the sun's rays and internal temperature.
The project also includes an internal pedestrian street, Plantation Lane, which cuts the site from east to west, from the church of St Margaret Pattens by Christopher Wren to Mincing Lane, enabling the two new buildings slot neatly into the historical context.

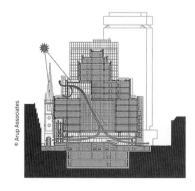

© Arup Associates

© Christian Richters

architects
Arup Associates

type
offices, public space

construction
2004

09. Lloyd's of London

1 Lime Street
London EC3M 7HA

Mon - Fri / 8 am - 6 pm

+44 (0) 20 73271000

www.lloyds.com

 Circle / District
Monument

In this famous piece of architecture by the Richard Rogers Partnership all the service areas – such as the 12 glass lifts and the stairs, but also the toilets and technological systems – are situated in six towers outside the actual building itself in order to maximise the interior space available for the offices. What is more, the structural parts form original decorative elements.

The building, 76 metres high, with a maximum of 14 floors above ground level, is organised around the large central atrium, the Underwriting Room, which is lit from above by an impressive glass barrel vault. A whole series of escalators span out from this space. These go up to the galleries on the first four floors, overlooking the atrium, while the upper floors can only be reached by the stairs and the external lifts.

The central body of the building is enclosed by a curtain cladding system consisting of three layers of special glass with a ventilated cavity wall, while the towers are finished with fireproof stainless steel panels.

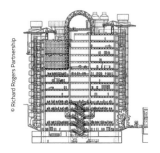

© Richard Rogers Partnership

architects
Richard Rogers Partnership

type
offices

construction
1986

10. The Leadenhall Building (The Cheesegrater)

122 Leadenhall Street
London EC3V 4AB

partly open to the public

+44 (0) 20 72208950

Circle / District
Monument

This singular skyscraper, which stands out against the City skyline, is nicknamed "The Cheesegrater" owing to its tapering form. Until 2007 the site was occupied by a 1960s building designed by the Gollins Melvin Ward Partnership, which was demolished to make way for the new tower, completed in 2014. The Leadenhall Building, with its 48 floors, reaches the height of around 225 metres, and no less than 70,000 square metres of glass were used to cover it. The surface area of the various levels varies from around 2,000 square metres on the first floors to around 550 at the top. The service areas, together with the stair and lift wells, are placed in a separate tower on the northern side. Even though the building occupies the whole site, the project envisaged the first seven floors. A public space was created at its base, a sort of gigantic portico that acts as a filter between the building and the congested surrounding area.

© Rogers Strik Harbour + Partners

© Marco Mughal

architects
Rogers Stirk Harbour +
Partners

type
offices

construction
2014

11. 30 St Mary Axe (The Gherkin)

30 St Mary Axe
London EC3A 8EP

partly open to the public

+44 (0) 20 70715029

www.30stmaryaxe.com

 Circle / Metropolitan
Aldgate

Originally known as the Swiss Re Building (named after the insurance group that first occupied the building) and ironically renamed by Londoners as "The Gherkin", ever since its completion this 41-floor, 180-metre-high building has become an icon on the city skyline.

Defined as "London's first ecological skyscraper", it was designed by adopting the most advanced energy-saving methods. Environmentally, its profile reduces wind deflections compared with a rectilinear tower of similar size, helping to maintain a comfortable environment at ground level, and creates external pressure differentials that are exploited to drive a unique system of natural ventilation. This allows its energy requirements to be reduced by around 50% of a conventional office tower. The glazed façade also allows natural light in, therefore also lowering lighting costs.

Thanks to the diagonally braced structure enveloping the whole façade no internal support pillars were needed, resulting large, column-free and flexible spaces for the offices. In addition to offices, the building also hosts shops on the ground floor and a top-floor restaurant.

© Foster + Partners

© Nigel Young/Foster + Partners

architects
Foster + Partners

type
retail, offices

construction
2004

12. Heron Tower

110 Bishopsgate
London EC2N 4AY

partly open to the public

**Central / Circle /
Hammersmith & City /
Metropolitan**
Liverpool Street

The skyscraper, which reaches a height of 230 metres, is in Bishopsgate, in the heart of the city, just a stone's throw from Liverpool Street Station. It offers over 40,000 square metres of office space, as well as a restaurant and a bar.

The Heron Tower was built according to the latest office building standards, with great attention to the quality of the materials and to detail. The building boasts a series of unique characteristics, amongst which the largest private aquarium in Great Britain. Situated in the reception area, it contains 1,200 fish of 67 different species.

The whole south face of the fully glazed building is covered in photovoltaic cells which, in addition to producing energy, create a shading effect which greatly reduces the need for air conditioning in the summer.

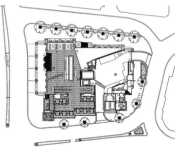

© Kohn Pedersen Fox Associates

architects
Kohn Pedersen Fox
Associates

type
offices

construction
2011

13. Principal Tower

2 Principal Place
London EC2A 2BA

external viewing only

www.principalplace.co.uk

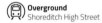

Overground
Shoreditch High Street

Principal Tower is the last element of a masterplan aimed at redeveloping all the surrounding area, and thanks to its segmented form and the materials employed, it recalls the historic cast iron industrial structures of Shoreditch, providing a sense of continuity in the urban landscape.

The 175 metre tower has 50 floors and is one of the tallest residential buildings in London. It is divided into three vertical elements; the centre tower rising higher than the side elements, creating a new landmark in this dynamic area of the city.

All the residents' facilities, like the gym, swimming pool, and bar on the mezzanine floor, have a strong link with the surrounding urban landscape, and have expansive views across the city. The apartments enjoy the same sweeping views thanks to the cruciform plan of the tower and the wide, full-height windows that maximise the natural light.

The architects paid special attention to reducing energy by incorporating different energy saving installations, including photovoltaic panels on the roof, and grey water harvesting systems.

© Foster + Partners

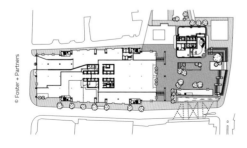

architects
Foster + Partners

type
residential

construction
2020

14. Angel Court

Angel Ct
London EC2R 7BH

external viewing only

angelcourtbank.com

**Central / Northern /
Waterloo & City**
Bank

This tower, with its unusual octagonal shape, replaces a 1970s office block, and takes its name from the narrow pedestrian street that leads to the building.

The tower's so-called "sky floors" are wrapped in a translucent skin that creates a continuous, homogeneous surface rising above the base structure composed of two six-storey buildings topped with roof gardens. These "garden floors" overlook the two side streets. The two elements are in striking contrast with one another: the tower has an ethereal, opalescent aspect created by the double ceramic frit glass façades that provide virtually transparent views from the interior whatever the light conditions, while the lower structures are clad in blocks of dark-coloured limestone.

The project also incorporated the creation of a new public space in the surrounding area, including the installation of seating and site-specific public art works.

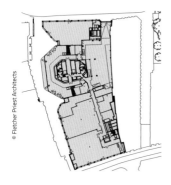

© Fletcher Priest Architects

architects
Fletcher Priest Architects

type
offices

construction
2017

15. London Wall Place

1-2 London Wall
London EC2Y 5AU

open to the public

www.londonwallplace.com

As well as the construction of two new office buildings, this project by Make Architects also include over an acre of public gardens and the restoration of fragments of ancient Roman city walls and the Medieval St Alphage church tower, both long-abandoned and previously not visible to the public. The intervention attained a triple objective: the recovery of the historic memory of the area, giving the city a series of beautifully designed green public spaces, and a faster connection between the Barbican Centre to the north and the City to the south. This was achieved by constructing suspended walkways that recall those built in the 1960s.

The two office blocks, 13 and 17 storeys high, feature contrasting bands of glass reinforced concrete, a special highly environmentally sustainable concrete, and dark blue ceramic ribbing, that form elongated vertical grids, in contrast with the strongly horizontal architecture of the Barbican Centre nearby. The two materials are inspired by the Kentish rag-stone found in the Roman walls. The GRC echoes the smooth opaque surface of the chalky exterior of the stone, while the iridescent blue ceramic recalls its shiny interior.

Circle / Hammersmith & City / Metropolitan / Northern
Moorgate

© Make Architects

© Make Architects

architects
Make Architects

type
offices, public space

construction
2017

16. The Barbican Complex

Silk Street
London EC2Y 8DS

partly open to the public

+44 (0) 20 76384141

www.barbican.org.uk

Circle / Hammersmith & City / Metropolitan
Barbican

This vast complex of buildings was built between 1969 and 1982 in an area that had been completely destroyed by bombing in the Second World War, and is named after a Roman fort in ancient Londinium thought to have been located on this site.

To date the Barbican is still the most important cultural and residential centre in the City. It houses two theatres, a multiscreen cinema, three restaurants, two art galleries (the Barbican Gallery and the Curve), the Barbican Hall, and the Barbican Estate, a residential complex consisting of 13 low-rise buildings and three high-rise towers, the Cromwell Tower, Shakespeare Tower and Lauderdale Tower.

The various bare concrete buildings are connected to each other by traffic-free communal areas, mainly laid out as gardens, dotted with artificial lakes.

© Leif Mendelsey

architects
Chamberlin, Powell & Bon

type
multi-purpose complex

construction
1982

17. 88 Wood Street

88 Wood Street
London EC2V 7RS

external viewing only

Central
St Paul's

This 33,000 square metres office building is situated on the site of a 1920s telephone exchange and was the first work completed in London by the Richard Rogers firm after Lloyd's of London. Between 1993 and 1999 its realisation was subject to complex negotiations, also because of the numerous planning restrictions in the area.

The building is organised into three interconnected blocks of varying heights. The lowest is the eight-floor building overlooking Wood Street, where two national monuments are found, ranging up to the 14 floors of the medium one and lastly the 18 floors of the tallest, on the side looking west towards London Wall, where higher buildings are found.

The building features two impressive fully glazed, steel service towers with a lightweight structure, containing toilets, lifts and stairs. All of the towers are connected on the ground floor by the large hall which crosses through the whole building, facilitating internal connections.

© Richard Rogers Partnership

© Marco Mugnai

architects
Richard Rogers Partnership

type
offices

construction
1999

18. Lloyds Banking Group Headquarters

25 Gresham Street
London EC2V 7HN

external viewing only

+44 (0) 20 76261500

www.lloydsbankinggroup.com

 Central
St Paul's

This compact office block, which appears to mediate between the contemporary buildings along London Wall and the Victorian edifices along Gresham Street, hosts ten floors of completely pillar-free, flexible workspace, as well as a fully glazed atrium and a basement level with a restaurant, storeroom and car park. Four panoramic lifts provide the connections to the upper floors.

The centre of the main façade presents a series of green terraces, while at the sides 30 mm-thick dark slate alternates with glass panels. In the interior, the latter correspond to the space that goes from desk level to a height of 2.2 metres from floor level; hence this provides sufficient lighting and an ample view from each work station.

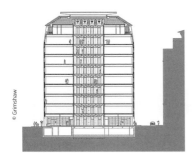

© Grimshaw

architects
Grimshaw

type
offices

construction
2002

19. Sixty London

60 Holborn Viaduct
London EC1A 2FD

partly open to the public

Central
St Paul's

Sixty London is a new, imposing, systematically shaped office building located on the Holborn Viaduct, in a strategic position between the City and the West End. The building stands out thanks to its unbroken steel-and-glass skin, marked by what the designers call 'fins', myriad vertical little wings that give the aspects rhythm. The project is unabashedly modern, as can be seen for example in the hundreds of glass panels, each of a different shape, and the while also incorporating historical aspects, such as the refurbished original Victorian-style lodge.

The building has some of the most advanced sustainability technology, such as solar-heated water and automatic light controls based on the light in the rooms. Hence, it has obtained BREEAM certification for environmental excellence.

© Kohn Pedersen Fox Associates

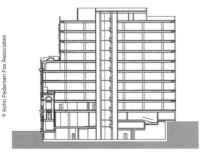

» Andrea Mugnai

architects
Kohn Pedersen Fox
Associates

type
retail, offices

construction
2013

20. New Ludgate

30 Old Bailey
London EC4M

partly open to the public

Central
St Paul's

It is a complex of two new office buildings that redesign a whole block situated a very short distance from St Paul's Cathedral. Previously on the site were buildings constructed in the 1980s. The masterplan and design of the first building, One New Ludgate is by Fletcher Priest Architects while Sauerbruch Hutton designed Two New Ludgate.

The master plan displays great attention towards the former history of the site and to defining the public space. It includes a passage between the two buildings, called Belle Sauvage in memory of a 15th-century inn found nearby, and a small square on the east side opposite an old Victorian building, offering a sunny area where workers can enjoy their lunch break.

The building by Fletcher Priest has a very solid appearance to create a sense of grandeur for the processional route to St Paul's. The façade features a regular white concrete grid while the side facing the square to the east is marked by amber-coloured glazing fins. Conversely, the building by Sauerbruch Hutton has a more 'playful' aspect, with coloured vertical partitions and a sleeker shape.

© Fletcher Priest Architects

© Tim Soar

architects
Fletcher Priest Architects +
Sauerbruch Hutton

type
retail, offices

construction
2015

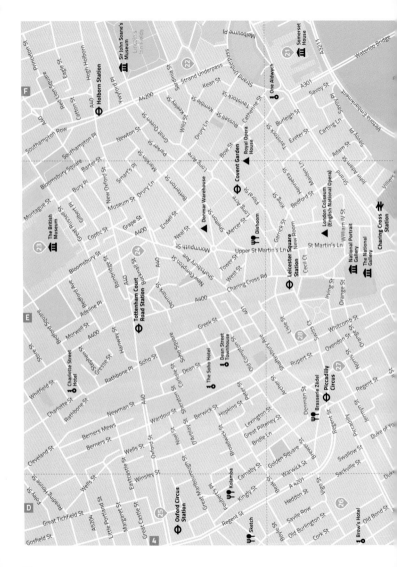

Lincoln's Inn Fields

Sir John Soane's Museum

Melbourne Pl

Somerset House

One Aldwych

Holborn Station

Strand Underpass

Royal Opera House

Covent Garden

Dishoom

Donmar Warehouse

The British Museum

London Coliseum (English National Opera)

Leicester Square Station

New Room

St Martin's Ln

National Portrait Gallery

The National Gallery

Charing Cross Station

Tottenham Court Road Station

Charlotte Street Hotel

Dean Street Townhouse

The Soho Hotel

Brasserie Zédel

Piccadilly Circus

Kolamba

Oxford Circus Station

Brow's Hotel

Sketch

70

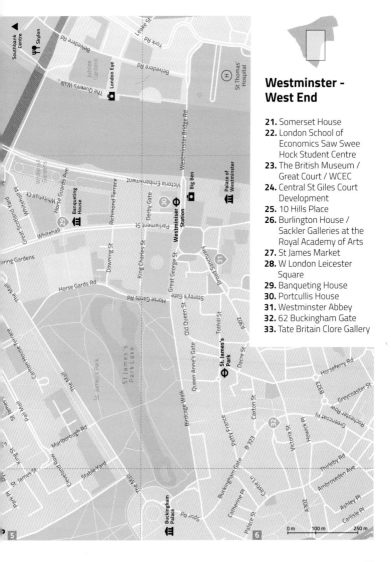

Westminster – West End

21. Somerset House
22. London School of Economics Saw Swee Hock Student Centre
23. The British Museum / Great Court / WCEC
24. Central St Giles Court Development
25. 10 Hills Place
26. Burlington House / Sackler Galleries at the Royal Academy of Arts
27. St James Market
28. W London Leicester Square
29. Banqueting House
30. Portcullis House
31. Westminster Abbey
32. 62 Buckingham Gate
33. Tate Britain Clore Gallery

0 m   100 m   250 m

21. Somerset House

Strand
London WC2R 1LA

Mon - Sat / 10 am - 6 pm
Sun / 2 pm - 6 pm

+44 (0) 20 78454600

www.somersethouse.org.uk

Circle / District
Temple

The main building is an elegant Palladian palace built in 1775 following the design of William Chambers. Planned to host some royal companies, it was then extended in the Victorian period with a north and a south wing. To make room for it, the existing Tudor style building built in 1547 on the banks of the River Thames for the Duke of Somerset was demolished.

Situated in the central area is the picturesque Edmond J. Safra Fountain Court, which was refurbished in 2000 with 55 fountains spouting from the ground. The courtyard hosts events in summer and an ice rink in winter.

Today the palace hosts two art galleries, the Courtauld Gallery, which houses an excellent collection of paintings by European masters, and the Embankment Galleries, which host exhibitions dedicated to architecture, photography, design and fashion.

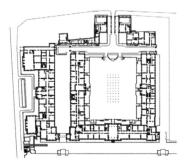

architects	type	construction
William Chambers	museum	1775

22. London School of Economics Saw Swee Hock Student Centre

1 Sheffield Street
London WC2A 2AP

partly open to the public

+44 (0) 20 71075420
s.ryan7@lse.ac.uk
sawsweehockcentre.com

Central / Piccadilly
Holborn

The project for this student centre came about from the desire to make the best possible use of the site, located at the heart of the tight web of small streets that typify the main London School of Economics campus. The façade of the building features sharp folds and rounded edges which give different viewpoints towards and from the surrounding context. At the points where the geometry changes, the red brick outer layer opens into large glazed surfaces linking the interior with the exterior.

The interior of this multi-purpose building, with its mixed iron and reinforced concrete structure, is laid out in a very intricate and flexible manner, to fit the dynamic nature of a modern student centre. Among other things, it hosts offices, a pub, a café, a gym, a dance lab and, above all, areas for meeting and socializing on all floors.

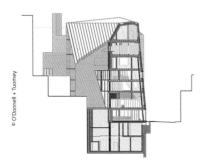

© O'Donnell + Tuomey

© Andrea Mugnai

architects
O'Donnell + Tuomey

type
student centre

construction
2014

23. The British Museum / Great Court / WCEC

Great Russell Street
London WC1B 3DG

Sat - Thu / 10 am - 5 pm
Fri / 10 am - 8.30 pm

+44 (0) 20 73238299
information@
britishmuseum.org
www.britishmuseum.org

Central / Northern
Tottenham Court Road

The museum, among the first in the world to be opened to the public (in 1759) is the city's most popular tourist destination, with an average of over 6 million visitors a year. The Neoclassical building which hosts it today was built in 1847 following the design of Robert Smirke, and thereafter extended on several occasions.

The Great Court, at the heart of the museum, is organised around the British Library's former Reading Room, currently used for temporary exhibitions, and is surrounded by various buildings which form its perimeter.

The court was renovated in 2000 by Foster + Partners, becoming the largest covered public square in Europe. The intervention consisted of covering the square with a light and flexible steel and glass structure that could adapt to the different forms of the surrounding buildings and at the same time allow as much natural light in as possible. The glass panels underwent a particular printing process to filter the light, and therefore help to make the interior space a comfortable temperature.

2014 saw the completion of one of the vastest renovation operations in the museum's history, with the creation of a new gallery in the north-western part of the complex designed by the Rogers Stirk Harbour + Partners firm. The new addition is called the "World Conservation and Exhibitions Centre".

© Foster + Partners

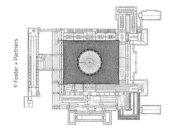

architects
Robert Smirke / Foster + Partners
/ Rogers Stirk Harbour + Partners

type
museum, public space

construction
1847 / 2000

24. Central St Giles Court Development

1-13 St Giles High Street
London WC2H 8AG

partly open to the public

Central / Northern
Tottenham Court Road

In 2001 Renzo Piano Building Workshop (RPBW) presented a master plan for Central St Giles, a site dominated by Centre Point, the imposing landmark designed by Richard Seifert in 1966.

The regeneration project, featuring bright-coloured buildings, blends in well with the lively Covent Garden, Bloomsbury and Soho districts.

The complex consists of two buildings – one residential, the other commercial – which outline a central courtyard accessible to the public via five pedestrian entrances. RPBW has divided the aspects so that it looks like a series of buildings side by side, each with a different façade, and coloured panels are used to create a pattern or impression of density. The building is set out over 10 floors around the internal courtyard which features a large oak tree, sculptures and pieces of urban furniture.

© Renzo Piano Building Workshop

architects
Renzo Piano Building Workshop
with Fletcher Priest Architects

type
offices, retail, residential,
public space

construction
2010

25. 10 Hills Place

10 Hills Place
London W1F 7SD

external viewing only

**Bakerloo / Central /
Victoria**
Oxford Circus

The building has an extremely distinctive sculpted façade. Like in a canvas by Lucio Fontana, each floor of the aspect is traversed by horizontal slashes of glass, pointing towards the sky to maximise the natural light available in the narrow street where the building is located.

This moulded shape is obtained using 140-millimetre-wide, curved aluminium profiles of the type customarily used in the production of hulls for luxury marine craft. They are connected together on-site, using a tongue-and-groove system for a watertight building with an efficient construction style. The high-performance paint used for the metallic silver finish also features in ship-building.

The façade is guaranteed low-maintenance thanks to the use of self-cleaning glass and an ingenious system of hidden gutters within the building's 'eyelids'.

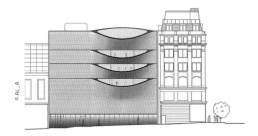

© AL_A

© Edmund Sumner

architects
AL_A

type
offices

construction
2009

26. Burlington House / Sackler Galleries at the Royal Academy of Arts

Piccadilly
London W1J 0BD

Thu - Sat / 10 am - 6 pm
Fri / 10 am - 10 pm

+44 (0) 20 73008000

 Bakerloo / Piccadilly
Piccadilly Circus

The building was constructed in 1668 for the first Count of Burlington and then renovated in 1712 in neo-Palladian style by Colen Campbell. In 1852, after undergoing further modifications, Burlington House was sold to the British government. Today it hosts important cultural institutions, amongst which the Royal Academy of Arts, famous for its collections and the exhibitions held there.
The work by Lord Norman Foster, completed in 1991, is the first, successful example of the architect's ability to insert clearly contemporary elements into historical contexts. The project set out to relocate the Diploma Galleries, make exhibition spaces for temporary exhibitions (the Sackler Galleries), and improve the interior communications, also by inserting stairs and lifts in the space between Burlington House itself and the Victorian building behind it. The project also included the renovation of the rear façade of Burlington House overlooking the beautiful garden, to regain its original appearance by eliminating all of the superfluous elements that had accumulated over time.

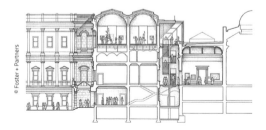

© Foster + Partners

© Andrea Mugnai

architects
Colen Campbell /
Foster + Partners

type
exhibition centre

construction
1668 / 1991

27. St James Market

2 St James's Market
London SW1Y 4AH

open to the public

+44 (0) 20 78515000
enquiries@thecrownestate.
co.uk
stjameslondon.co.uk

Bakerloo / Piccadilly
Piccadilly Circus

The aim of this project was to revitalise an area immediately south of Piccadilly Circus, known as St James's Market, a site rich in history hidden in the heart of Westminster that had been lost and forgotten following the construction of Regent Street.

The intervention involved the restoration of a late 19th century building that overlooks Regent Street St James's, and the construction of a new office and retail building opposite. The new building features curving horizontal bands of Portland stone inlaid with strips of bronze. The unifying aspect of the project lies in the use of the same façade materials, and highlighted by the tall bronze portals, seven and a half metres high, at the ground floor entrances of both buildings.

A new central public space is designed to draw people into the heart of the scheme, where the cafes and restaurants spill out. It plays host to events and has a permanent arts pavilion showing works by London artists.

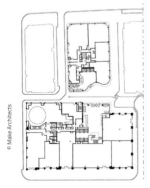

© Make Architects

architects	type	construction
Make Architects	retail, offices	2017

28. W London Leicester Square

10 Wardour Street
London W1D 6QF

partly open to the public

+44 (0) 20 77581000
wleicestersquare@
reservestarwood.com
www.wlondon.co.uk

🚇 **Nothern / Piccadilly**
Leicester Square

The W London hotel in Leicester Square provides a new landmark for the Soho district in the West End of London. In addition to the hotel, the building hosts shops, apartments and a wellbeing centre over a total surface area of 200.000 square metres.

The convex façade is clad in suspended translucent glass and looks like the folds of a theatre curtain, highlighting the cinematographic connections of this part of the West End.

The aspect is like an enormous screen that can project moving light installations during the hours of darkness.

The interiors, designed by Concrete Architectural Associates, have been devised to offer guests a rapid but all-in experience of London design culture. The mix of traditional and contemporary materials creates spaces that are both comfortable and futuristic at the same time.

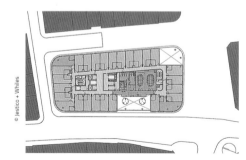

© Jestico + Whiles

© Hufton+Crow

architects
Jestico + Whiles

type
hotel

construction
2011

29. Banqueting House

Whitehall
London SW1A 2ER

Mon - Sun / 10 am - 5 pm

+44 (0) 20 31666155

Circle / District / Jubilee
Westminster

Banqueting House, first and foremost example of Renaissance architecture in England, was commissioned by James I and designed by Inigo Jones. The building, whose name derives from the banquet hall, completed in 1622, with coffered ceiling adorned by paintings by Rubens, replaces the previous royal residence of Whitehall, destroyed by a fire in 1619.

The stone façade, comprising Ionic and Corinthian orders (bottom and top respectively), is modelled after the Palladian prototypes that Jones had been able to study during his travels to Italy. The lower windows are surmounted by alternating curved and pointed pediments, while the upper windows are casements.

The Renaissance classical ideals are even more evident in the interior. The large hall has the shape and proportions of two cubes (110×55×55 metres), following the classical rules for the composition of a Roman basilica.

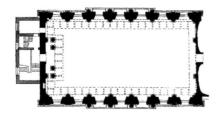

architects
Inigo Jones

type
museum

construction
1622

30. Portcullis House

Bridge Street
London SW1A 2LW

external viewing only

0844 8471672 (UK)
+44 (0) 161 4258677
(from abroad)

www.parliament.uk

**Circle / District /
Jubilee**
Westminster

The new seat of Parliament, situated along the Thames adjacent to the historic Palace of Westminster, hosts the MPs' offices as well as committee rooms. The building has a compact rectangular outline and is six storeys high. The façades have special shutters to store energy as well as to filter the natural light.

Restaurants and the library overlook the central courtyard, the pivotal point of the whole building, whose spectacular glass vaulted roof is supported by a mesh of American white oak laminated timber. The roof rests on just six pillars and is based on a netted structure which includes glass panels tracing a constant curve. Designed by the Arup engineering firm, it is one of the most complex structures of its kind in Europe, creating a space sheltered against bad weather but generously lit by natural light.

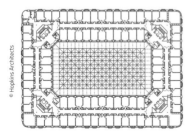

© Hopkins Architects

architects
Hopkins Architects,
Arup Associates

type
offices

construction
2000

31. Westminster Abbey

20 Deans Yard
London SW1P 3PA

Mon - Sun / 9.30 am - 6 pm

+44 (0) 20 72225152
info@westminster-abbey.org
www.westminster-abbey.org

Circle / District / Jubilee
Westminster

Although it is supposed that the abbey's foundation dates as far back as the 7th century, the present church, masterpiece of early English Gothic reworked numerous times over the centuries, was consecrated in 1269. The interior, with three naves and tall sheaved pillars, preserves the majesty of the Gothic structure and is host to the Sacrarium, site of the British monarchs' coronations, weddings and funerals. The main altar, standing over an original Cosmati pavement, was designed by George Gilbert Scott in 1873.

The late-Gothic apsidal chapel was added in 1519 by Henry VII. This three-aisled structure with side houses the splendid bronze tombs of past royals. In addition to 17 royals, the church is the burial place of numerous illustrious personalities from English history.

Organized around a majestic cloister, the abbey is also host to a magnificent octagonal chapter house with the vault supported by a single central pillar and the original Medieval floor. Another feature is the Pyx Chamber which houses the cathedral's treasury.

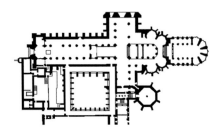

© Mauro Sampaolesi

architects	type	construction
-	church	1269

32. 62 Buckingham Gate

62 Buckingham Gate
London SW1E 6PA

external viewing only

+44 (0) 20 74936040

www.62bg.com

Circle / District
St James's Park

The large building at number 62 Buckingham Gate is a new landmark building made entirely of glass at the crossroads with Victoria Street. It hosts over 2,000 square metres of office space distributed over 11 floors, and almost 1,500 square metres of retail space on the ground floor. Completed in spring 2013, the building was designed by the Pelli Clarke Pelli Architects firm along with executive architects Swanke Hayden Connell and interior designers Lehman Smith McLeish (LSM).

The project paid great attention to aspects of sustainability, which, among other things, led to the realisation of a green roof and the use of highly energy-efficient cladding.

The horizontal stripes on the façade, made of anodised bronze, blend with the colours of the surrounding Victorian and Edwardian buildings.

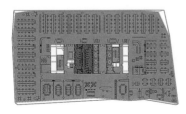

architects
Pelli Clarke Pelli Architects

type
retail, offices

construction
2013

33. Tate Britain Clore Gallery

Millbank
London SW1P 4RG

Mon - Sun / 10 am - 6 pm

+44 (0) 20 79834000
visiting.modern@tate.org.uk
www.tate.org.uk

 Victoria
Pimlico

The Clore Gallery, completed in 1986 and opened the following year, is an extension of the historic museum devoted to British art, hosted in Sidney Smith's Neoclassical building since 1897. It is considered an eminent example of Postmodern architecture, in particular owing to its 'contextual irony'; indeed, citations from the original building can be found at various points of the façade, visible both in the compositional details and in the materials used.

The new gallery by Stirling and Wilford has an L-shaped floor plan and hosts the vast Turner Collection of paintings, water colours, sketches and drawings by the English painter William Turner. After its opening, the Clore Gallery sparked a heated debate since many considered the building, devised as a 'work of art' itself, unsuitable for hosting the great artist's paintings.

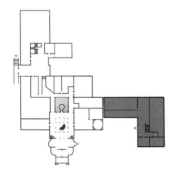

© Giacomo Carpini

architects
James Stirling and Associates
/ Michael Wilford and
Associates

type
museum

construction
1986

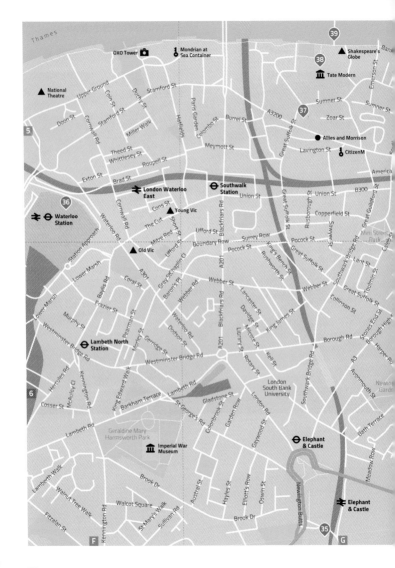

Thames

OXO Tower

Mondrian at
Sea Container

National
Theatre

Upper Ground

Coin St

Stamford St

Duchy St

Doon St

Stamford St

Cornwall Rd

Miller Walk

Hatfields

Paris Gardens

Colombo St

Burrel St

A3200

Sumner St

Sumner St

Zoar St

Emerson St

Shakespeare's
Globe

Tate Modern

39

38

37

Great Suffolk St

Allies and Morrison

Lavington St

CitizenM

America

B300

Theed St

Whittlesey St

Roupell St

Meymott St

Exton St

Brad St

Cornwall Rd

Waterloo Rd

London Waterloo
East

Cons St

The Cut

Mitre Rd

Short St

Ufford St

Young Vic

Boundary Row

Southwalk
Station

Union St

Surrey Row

Blackfriars Rd

Great Suffolk St

Union St

Rushworth St

Copperfield St

Great Guildford St

36

Waterloo
Station

Old Vic

Ufford St

Pocock St

Pocock St

King's Bench St

Great Suffolk St

Southwark Bridge Rd

Lant St

Mini Street
Park

Station Approach

Lower Marsh

Coral St

Baylis Rd

Frazier St

Pearman St

Gray St

Chaplin Cl

Baron's Pl

Webber St

Webber St

Webber St

Lancaster St

Dolben St

Mirom St

King James St

Collinson St

Great Suffolk St

Borough Rd

Toulmin St

Stones End St

Borough High St

Lower Marsh

Murphy St

Westminster Bridge Rd

Lambeth North
Station

Morton St

Gerridge St

Doughton St

Waterloo Rd

A201

Blackfriars Rd

Library St

Rotary St

Keil St

London
South Bank
University

Southwark Bridge Rd

Harper Rd

A3

Hercules Rd

Kennington Rd

D'Aubigny Rd

Westminster Bridge Rd

King Edward Walk

Barkham Terrace

Lambeth Rd

Gladstone St

St George's Rd

Colombord St

Garden Row

London Rd

Ipswood St

Elephant
& Castle

Avonmouth Rd

Newing
Garden

Bath Terrace

6

Cosser St

Lambeth Rd

Geraldine Mary
Harmsworth Park

Imperial War
Museum

Brook Dr

Austral St

Hayles St

Elliott's Row

Oswin St

Cataword St

Newington Butts

Meadow Row

Elephant
& Castle

Lambeth Walk

Walnut Tree Walk

Walcot Square

St. Mary's Walk

Sullivan Rd

Brook Dr

35

Fitzalan St

Kennington Rd

F

G

98

South Bank - Greenwich - South London

34. Vauxhall Cross Bus Station

Bondway
London SW8 1SJ

open to the public

Victoria
Vauxhall

The new Vauxhall Cross bus station, designed by Arup following a competition launched by Transport for London in 2002, tidies up a square that previously had no points of reference. Hence the canopy has a strong sculpted appearance, the high and low parts of its metallic structure forming the stopping and waiting areas. The northern part of the roof rises up towards the sky like a ski slope; it is not just for impact, but is of absolute substance, since the roof supports numerous integrated photovoltaic cells which, pointing towards the sun, generate the electrical current needed to light up the station. The 'green' energy supply was a central aspect of the project and, to keep passengers constantly informed of this, a digital display shows the quantity of solar energy used by the structure.

© Arup Associates

architects
Arup Associates

type
bus station

construction
2005

35. Strata SE1

8 Walworth Road
London SE1 6SX

external viewing only

www.stratalondon.com

Bakerloo / Northern
Elephant & Castle

This show-stopping round building is located in a once quite degraded area of South Bank. However, it has recently been regenerated thanks to the opening of this futuristic cinema, as well as the new pedestrian zone, a café and the installation of a large work by the well-known artist Howard Hodgkin.

The cinema is located, surrounded by traffic lanes, right in the centre of the large roundabout between Waterloo Road, Stamford Street and York Road, as well as above two Tube lines. The designers therefore wanted to protect the cinema hall from noise and disturbance from the outside, and so placed the structure on special vibration-proof and noise-proof cushions.

Built for the British Film Institute in 1999, the Imax seats around 500 and, at 20 metres tall and 26 wide, has the largest screen in the United Kingdom.

© Hamilton Architects

architects
Hamilton Architects

type
residential

construction
2010

36. Waterloo International Terminal

Waterloo Road
London SE1 7LT

open to the public

Bakerloo / Jubilee /
Northern / Waterloo
& City
Waterloo

This aerodynamic structure, known as the "Gateway to Europe" is an ultramodern multifunctional transport hub built right next door to the historic Waterloo Station, on a site just wide enough to host the five tracks required by the project. Its long and sleek form – with an irregular width varying between 34 and 50 metres – made it necessary for a very hi-tech asymmetrical roof design. The roof is a low, triple-lock arch shape with a cover made of different materials, the west side of which is totally glazed.
The inside of the station is divided into two levels, one for arrivals, and one for departures, like an airport, in order to facilitate the enormous flow of passengers as far as possible. The two levels are linked by glass escalators and moving walkways.

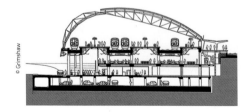

© Grimshaw

architects
Grimshaw

type
railway station

construction
1993

37. Bankside 123

110 Southwark Street
London SE1 0SU

external viewing only

Jubilee
Southwark

The construction of this three-office building complex – an extension of the nearby City – along the south bank of the Thames also provided the opportunity to create new public, commercial and cultural spaces which have fostered the urban regeneration of the whole surrounding area.

The buildings are simple parallel forms. Each adapts to the site with its particular floor plan, leading to interesting geometric variations in the conformation of the ground-floor public spaces.

The completely glazed façades in the first building (known as the Blue Fin Building) are shaded by vertical aluminium wings, while the other two feature earthenware ceramic panels alongside each window.

© Allies and Morrison

architects
Allies and Morrison

type
offices

construction
2010

38. Tate Modern

Bankside
London SE1 9TG

Sun - Thu / 10 am - 6 pm
Fri - Sat / 10 am - 10 pm

+44 (0) 20 78878888
visiting.modern@tate.org.uk
www.tate.org.uk

Jubilee
Southwark

The Tate Modern is situated on the banks of the Thames inside the red-brick former Bankside Power Station, which closed down in 1981. The original building, 200 metres long and with a 99-metre tall chimney, was renovated following the competition launched in 1994, won by Herzog & de Meuron.

The only external modification was the addition of a two-storey glass structure on the roof. The most spectacular space in the building is without doubt the former Turbine Hall, a sort of large covered square which the public can enter free of charge. Providing an entrance hall to the galleries, it hosts displays which are changed periodically. Light plays a determining role in defining the interior spaces and in the interpretation of the works of art. The natural light that filters through the large windows alternates cleverly with the artificial lighting from glass panels in the ceiling. In addition to the exhibition rooms set out over seven floors, the Tate Modern hosts offices, a bookshop, a restaurant, classrooms and an auditorium.

An extension to the museum, again designed by Herzog & de Meuron, was opened in 2016. Named the "Blavatnik Building", with its brick cladding it seeks to blend in with the original structure in spite of its irregular shape.

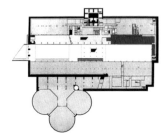

architects
Herzog & de Meuron

type
museum

construction
1995-2000 /
2005-2016 (extension)

39. Millennium Bridge

Millennium Bridge
London SE1

open to the public

Circle / District
Mansion House

Millennium Bridge is the first bridge to have been built over the Thames in central London since Tower Bridge. The idea was to make a light and linear structure that did not blot out the view over the river. The result is a sleek steel blade, dramatically lit up at night from below.

Slung as low as possible over the river, the bridge totals 320 metres in length (with a central span of 144 metres) and is extra slim, thanks to the use of innovative technologies. The structure is held up by eight prestressed steel cables anchored to the banks by deep reinforced concrete pillars, while the deck is supported by steel transverse arms clamped onto the cables at 8-metre intervals. The two slender middle pillars are elliptical in shape.

As is well-known, two days after it was opened, the bridge was closed owing to excessive lateral movement. After careful testing, the Arup engineering team designed dampers situated at various points in the structure to mitigate the sway, which has resulted in changes to the codes for bridge building worldwide.

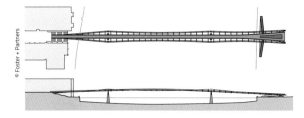

© Foster + Partners

architects
Foster + Partners, Antony
Caro, Arup Associates

type
bridge

construction
2000

40. London Bridge Station

20 Stainer Street
London SE1 9RL

open to the public

+44 (0) 34 57484950

 Northern / Jubilee
London Bridge

The London Bridge Station, opened in 1836, is the oldest railway station in London. It was completely renovated after the decision to make it the central hub of Thameslink, the railway system connecting several London counties with the cities of Bedford to the north and Brighton, to the south.

The new station cleverly combines original Victorian structures with radical contemporary design, and is built on two levels. At ground level is a vast, triple height concourse: an enormous covered public plaza linked directly with the adjacent skyscraper, The Shard, that houses all the station services. The railway tracks and platforms are on the upper floor, with canopies composed of long steel bands along the entire platforms, that allow daylight to penetrate the lower floor.

As well as representing an iconic national reference point, the new infrastructural hub provides a further advantage. At local level, it has opened up the area reconnecting the adjacent London neighbourhoods of Bankside-Borough and Bermondsey, that had been isolated from one another for decades.

© Paul Raftery

architects
Grimshaw

type
railway station

construction
2018

41. London Bridge Tower (The Shard)

32 London Bridge Street
London SE1 9SG

partly open to the public

+44 (0) 844 4997111
press@theviewfromtheshard.com
www.londonbridgequarter.com

Jubilee / Northern
London Bridge

At approximately 310 metres high, when it was completed the London Bridge Tower, nicknamed "The Shard", was the tallest skyscraper in Europe.

To try to make it as light as possible, the building tapers greatly towards the summit, like a sort of pyramid, and is entirely clad in hi-tech glass panels. The central core of the structure is made of reinforced concrete and hosts no less than 44 lifts. A scrupulous air-conditioning system enables 30% energy savings compared to a conventional building. In some points of the building winter gardens recreate small natural environments indoors.

The building, which can hold up to 7,000 people at the same time, houses offices, various restaurants, a luxury hotel, shops and exclusive apartments on the top floors. The only things above these are spectacular public viewing galleries situated between the 68th and 72nd floors.

Next door to the skyscraper is another more compact, squat building, completed the following year, London Bridge Place.

© Renzo Piano Building Workshop

architects
Renzo Piano Building Workshop
with Adamson Associates

type
residential, offices, retail,
hotel, public space

construction
2012

42. London City Hall

The Queens Walk
London SE1 2AA

Mon - Thu / 8.30 am - 6 pm
Fri / 8.30 am - 5 pm

+44 (0) 20 79834000

www.london.gov.uk

 Jubilee / Northern
London Bridge

The headquarters of the Greater London Authority is part of a wider programme to regenerate the More London area on the south bank of the Thames opposite the Tower of London, which, among other things, hosts a series of office buildings built by Foster + Partners.

City Hall includes the seat of the London Assembly, administrative offices, a public library and some restaurants. The building's unusual spherical shape stems from the goal to maximise its environmental sustainability. Indeed, as a result, the building has a 25% smaller surface area than a cube of the same volume and, in addition to requiring less building materials, a smaller surface area is exposed to direct sunlight, meaning great energy savings, also boosted by the use of glass of different opacity depending on the position of the panes.

The interior space is characterised by a long spiral staircase that climbs up to the top of the building, where an area open to the public becomes a privileged point for observing the city skyline, as well as following the assembly sessions held below.

© Foster + Partners

116

© Nigel Young/Foster + Partners

architects
Foster + Partners

type
offices, public space

construction
2002

43. Old Royal Naval College

King William Walk
London SE10 9NN

Mon - Sun / 10 am - 5 pm

+44 (0) 20 82694799
info@ornc.org
www.ornc.org

DLR
Cutty Sark for
Maritime Greenwich

The building originated in 1692 on the site of the previous Old Palace of Placentia, when Christopher Wren received a royal commission to design a hospital for sailors, which was then transformed into the Royal Naval College in 1869. Wren decided to arrange the buildings on either side of a large central avenue, in order not to block the view of the Thames from the Queen's House by Inigo Jones located immediately to the south.

Standing out within the complex is Saint Peter and Paul's chapel, designed in the 18th century by James "Athenian" Stuart and William Newton, its rich decorations somewhere between Greek Neoclassicism and Rococo style. Then there is the Painted Hall, with its sumptuous architecture and paintings, originally a dining room for sailors, but which soon became a ceremonial space for special events.

Today it is the site of the University of Greenwich and the Trinity College of Music, with two rooms open to the public.

architects
Christopher Wren

type
multi-purpose building

construction
1692-1712

44. Laban Dance Centre (Laban Building)

Creekside
London SE8 3DZ

partly open to the public

+44 (0) 20 83054444

www.trinitylaban.ac.uk

DLR
Cutty Sark for
Maritime Greenwich

This large dance centre, named after the famous choreographer Rudolf Laban, is located in Deptford Creekside, an area of the city characterised by warehouses and factories which has been undergoing regeneration since the early 2000s. The structure includes a theatre, 13 dance studios, a library, an archive and a bar.

The unbroken curved façade is clad with special polycarbonate panels that react to the sun's rays; during the day, depending on the curve, the building changes colour, with shades that go from translucent white to turquoise and magenta.

The sleek façade is in contrast to the complex interior, set out around the theatre centrepiece. The designers have organised the various activities inside this irregular box as if it were a small urban space, with streets, squares, common areas and private rooms.

The façade's double skin creates a subtle relationship between the interior and exterior. The façades filter the effects of the movements of the people inside the building as well as the effects generated by the decorations on the walls.

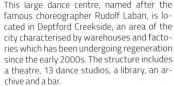

© Tim Hocker

architects
Herzog & de Meuron

type
dance centre

construction
2003

45. Royal Observatory Greenwich

Blackheath Avenue
London SE10 8XJ

Mon - Sun / 10 am - 5 pm

+44 (0) 20 88584422

www.rmg.co.uk/royal-observatory

DLR
Cutty Sark for
Maritime Greenwich

The project by Allies and Morrison includes the construction of a new planetarium, the transformation of the nineteenth-century south part of the complex and the landscaping of all the external areas of the UNESCO heritage site.

The south part of the complex, unused for some time, has taken on a renewed central role by locating all the new visitor services there, amongst which a shop and coffee shop. A new paved stone courtyard has been created at the southern end, surrounded by the trees of Greenwich Park.

In this updated context, the new planetarium is enclosed in an inclined, truncated bronze cone, its geometry defined by the complex relationship between its location – latitude and longitude – and the universe it represents on the inside. For example, its slant aligns it with the pole star, while the top surface is parallel to the celestial equator.

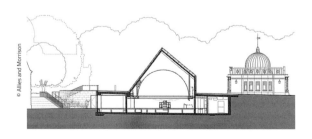

© Allies and Morrison

© Dennis Gilbert

architects
Allies and Morrison

type
astronomical observatory

construction
2007

46. Millennium Dome (The O2)

Peninsula Square
London SE10 0DX

open to the public

+44 (0) 20 84632000
info@theo2.co.uk
www.theo2.co.uk

 Jubilee
North Greenwich

Large, iconic and impactful dome-shaped building situated along the Greenwich meridian line, the Millennium Dome was a key element in the development of the master plan for the peninsula and prompted an enormous public debate during and after its construction.

Since June 2005 known as "The O2" after the telephone company which acquired its rights, it was designed to offer a large indoor exhibition space on occasion of the celebrations for the new millennium. Built following the principles of flexibility, lightness, construction speed and low cost, the Dome has a surface area of 100,000 square metres, a circumference of around one kilometre, a diameter of 365 metres and a maximum height of 50 metres. The structure is supported by twelve 100-metre-tall steel poles. In the centre it hosts the "O2 Arena", a multi-purpose hall for performances, concerts and sports events.

© Richard Rogers Partnership

architects
Richard Rogers Partnership

type
multi-purpose centre

construction
1999

47. Ravensbourne College

6 Penrose Way
London SE10 0EW

partly open to the public

+44 (0) 20 30403500
info@rave.ac.uk
www.ravensbourne.ac.uk

Jubilee
North Greenwich

The ultra-technological building which hosts the headquarters of this specialist innovative design and digital media research institute is situated on the central axis of the Greenwich Peninsula Masterplan, right opposite Richard Rogers' Millennium Dome.
The façade has a distinctive floral motif cladding, alternating with circular hollow spaces of seven different sizes (inspired by 'Gothic rose windows' according to the designers), all made using just three tile formats. The result is a psychedelic and innovative pattern, which enables a remarkable degree of transparency and permeability between the exterior and interior. The latter is organized around two connected collective areas. These are directly linked to all the levels of the building, in order to promote collaboration and the exchange of knowledge between the different cultural and professional figures working in the college.
Thanks to its use of the most advanced construction technologies, the building has obtained BREEAM environmental certification.

© FOA

© Marco Mugnai

architects	type	construction
Foreign Office Architects	research centre	2010

48. Peninsula Place

14 Pier Walk, 6 Mitre Passage
London SE10 0ES

partly open to the public

+44 (0) 20 30403500

 Jubilee
North Greenwich

The complex is divided into two buildings, Building A (14 Pier Walk) to the north and Building B (6 Mitre Passage) to the south, which fit into the general master plan for the area, creating a strong visual impact on the square. The concept envisaged bodies which apparently slide into each other, like 'blades' separated by a walkway that divides the two buildings and creates a linear route from one part of the complex to the other. The design of the façades is inspired by Paul Klee's painting, *Fire in the Evening* from 1929, giving the image of a sort of irregular modular tapestry, created with coloured glass panels.

Building A gets up to a height of 8 storeys, with an overall surface area of over 26,000 square metres, while Building B goes up 13 floors, with a total surface area of around 16,000 square metres. The complex was designed following eco-sustainability criteria and hosts offices and shops.

architects
Farrells

type
offices, retail

construction
2008

49. Evelyn Grace Academy

255 Shakespeare Road
London SE24 0QN

partly open to the public

+44 (0) 20 77379520
info@evelyngraceacademy.org
www.evelyngraceacademy.org

 Victoria
Brixton

The Evelyn Grace Academy, located in the historic borough of Lambeth in south London, is the building that enabled Zaha Hadid to win the Stirling Prize for the second year in a row. The complex consists of four schools, each with its own identity, which share common services and areas. The order was to create two secondary schools and two colleges for 1,200 pupils, equipped with various playing fields and a running track owing to the complex's specialisation in sport as well as mathematics and science.

Hadid chose to pack the four schools into a single, open, transparent and recognisable building. The aim is to stitch together the surrounding tattered urban fabric with a sleek shape that curves between two large roads. The building slots around a central axis comprising a 100-metre track which the building literally straddles, like a bridge. The façade has hi-tech cladding, following the project outlines.

© Zaha Hadid Architects

© Edmund Sumner

architects
Zaha Hadid Architects

type
school

construction
2010

50. Battersea Power Station Redevelopment

188 Kirtling Street
London SW8 5BN

partly open to the public

+44 (0) 20 75010688
info@batterseapowerstation.
co.uk
batterseapowerstation.co.uk

London Overground
Battersea Park

The Battersea Power Station, designed in 1933, and definitively decommissioned in 1983, is one of the icons of English industrial architecture. Today it is the heart of an ambitious urban redevelopment plan that covers a 42 acre area. The current work began in 2013, with estimated completion in 2025. The master-plan, to be built in several stages, is aimed at creating a new ecologically sustainable district, and was designed in 2010 by the Viñoly architectural firm.

At present, the first three phases have been completed or are under construction. Phase 1 includes the residential area of Circus West Village, with Faraday house, the RS1-B building (dRMM), and the RS1-A building (SimpsonHaugh and Partners), complete with large outdoor leisure areas and landscaping (LDA Design); Phase 2 refers to the restoration of the historic Power Station itself, (Purcell group), the expansion of the original building, (WilkinsonEyre) and the creation of the Power Station Park (LDA Design); Phase 3 involves the construction of residential housing south of the original structure, and includes the Battersea Roof Garden building, Electric Boulevard (Foster + Partners), the Prospect Place complex, Prospect Park (Gehry Partners) and the Malaysia square (BIG group).

© WilkinsonEyre

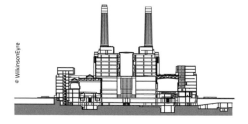

architects
Sir Giles Gilbert Scott / Rafael
Viñoly Architects (masterplan)

type
multi-purpose building

construction
1933 / 2020

51. Montevetro

100 Battersea Church Road
London SW11 3YL

external viewing only

 London Overground
Clapham Junction

This residential building on the banks of the Thames comprises five blocks of increasing height, from the first 4-storey building facing the church of St Mary, to the 20-floor block facing the river at the north-western extremity. The blocks are connected by the lift and stair wells. As well as strongly outlining the eastern profile of the building, where earthenware cladding alternates with the windows these enable direct access to each of the 103 flats without having to use internal corridors. The large glazed surfaces of the west aspect give the dwellings a beautiful view towards the river and the Chelsea district, as far as West London. The project also included the creation of a park along the river, between Wandsworth Bridge and Battersea Bridge.

© Richard Rogers Partnership

© Andrea Majgnal

architects
Richard Rogers Partnership

type
residential

construction
2000

52. Burntwood School

Burntwood Lane
London SW17 0AQ

partly open to the public

+44 (0) 20 89466201
info@burntwoodschool.com
www.burntwoodschool.com

 Northern
Tooting Broadway

The complex comes about from the renovation and extension of a 1950s Modernist school campus situated in south-west London. The main aim of the project was to renew the campus by producing a cohesive and uniform image, with lawns, squares and a central walkway. All the existing buildings in the complex were restored and modernised, with the addition of four pavilions for classrooms, a new sports hall and a new arts building.

The inside of each building is split up into double-height rooms, along a central corridor, in order to maximise the natural light. The intricate and dynamic façade comprises multifaceted prefabricated concrete panels, each corresponding to a 7.5-metre structural module. The complex won the RIBA Stirling Prize in 2015 for the architects' ability to combine a contemporary architectural image with the reuse of existing buildings, their attention to landscape aspects and use of prefabricated concrete modular elements, which highlights the attention towards sustainability in the construction process too.

© Allford Hall Monaghan Morris

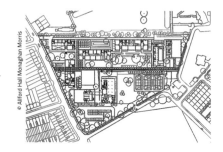

©Andrea Mughai

architects
Allford Hall Monaghan Morris

type
school

construction
2014

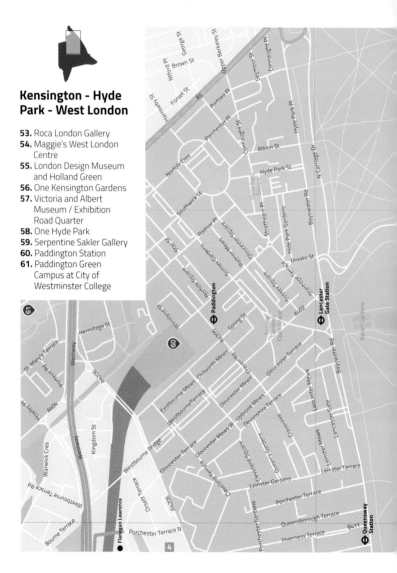

Kensington - Hyde Park - West London

53. Roca London Gallery
54. Maggie's West London Centre
55. London Design Museum and Holland Green
56. One Kensington Gardens
57. Victoria and Albert Museum / Exhibition Road Quarter
58. One Hyde Park
59. Serpentine Sakler Gallery
60. Paddington Station
61. Paddington Green Campus at City of Westminster College

0 m   100 m   250 m

The Royal Parks

Hi-de Park

The Serpentine

W. Carriage Dr

S Carriage Dr

58

59

Kensington Gardens

Round Pond

Kensington Palace

Princes Gate Garden

Basil St

Knightsbridge

Raphael St

Lancelot Pl

Trevor Square

Trevor Pl

Montpelier St

Montpelier Square

Rutland Gardens

Montpelier Walk

Rutland Gate

Rutland Gate

Rutland St

Princes Gate

Ennismore Mews

Ennismore Gardens

Ennismore Gardens

Ennismore Gardens Mews

Princes Gate

S Carriage Dr

A315

Princes Gardens

Princes Gardens

Princes Gate Mews

57 **Victoria and Albert Museum**

Oratory Gardens

Brompton Rd

Hans Rd

Brompton Pl

Beaufort Gardens

Ovington Gardens

Yeoman's Row

Walton St

Cheval Pl

Brompton Square

Brompton Rd

Cottage Pl

Exhibition Rd

Exhibition Rd

Science Museum

Natural History Museum

Royal Albert Hall

Ayrton Rd

Prince Consort Rd

Ayrton Rd

Imperial College Rd

Frankland Rd

Museum Ln

A315

Callendar Rd

Wells Way

Jay Mews

Queen's Gate

Queen's Gate

Hide Park Gate

Hyde Park Gate

Gore St

Queen's Gate Terrace

Elvaston Pl

Queen's Gate Gardens

Kensington Gate

Launceston Place

Petersham Ln

Palace Gate

Gloucester Rd

De Vere Gardens

Launceston Pl

Victoria Rd

Victoria Rd

Cornwall Gardens

56

C

B

A

5

6

53. Roca London Gallery

Townmead Road
London SW6 2PY

Mon - Fri / 9 am - 5 pm
Sat / 11 am - 5 pm

+44 (0) 20 76109503
info.londongallery@roca.net
www.rocalondongallery.com

 London Overground
Imperial Wharf

The gallery, originating as the showroom for the products of Roca, leading company in the bathroom fixtures and furnishings sector, hosts a vast range of activities, such as presentations, meetings, debates and seminars. Zaha Hadid's design is inspired by the force of water, which fluidly defines and sculpts both the external and internal spaces. The three portals giving access to the showroom, for example, almost seem to be a work of nature and appear to have been modelled by water erosion. The interiors, set out on a single floor, occupying a surface area of 1,100 square metres, are made of polished white concrete with highly sophisticated audiovisual equipment and advanced light and sound systems. The Roca London Gallery received the New London Award 2013, the prize for the architectural quality of the buildings built in the English capital.

© Zaha Hadid Architects

© Hufton+Crow

architects
Zaha Hadid Architects

type
exhibition centre

construction
2011

54. Maggie's West London Centre

Fulham Palace Road
London W6 8RF

external viewing only

+44 (0) 20 73861750

www.maggiescentres.org

**District / Circle /
Hammersmith & City /
Piccadilly**
Hammersmith

Maggie's West London was the first Maggie's cancer support centre to be built in London. Designed by Rogers Stirk Harbour + Partners, was inaugurated in 2008. The idea was to create a welcoming, familiar and comfortable shelter, a sort of protective shell that reduced the visual impact of the adjacent Charing Cross hospital to a minimum. The concept is a traditional house, as can be seen first of all with the kitchen area in the centre of the building and the inclusion of three fireplaces, the classic symbol of domestic warmth.

Orange walls welcome visitors into spaces which are light-filled and open thanks to flexible mobile walls.

The building is made up of four basic elements: a wall enclosing it on four sides, protecting it from the outside; a kitchen with a double-height central space that acts as the fulcrum and heart of the building; rooms annexed to the main space, designed for meetings, sessions and consultancy; and a roof which seems to float above the perimeter wall.

© Rogers Stirk Harbour + Partners

Caterina Frisone

architects
Rogers Stirk Harbour +
Partners

type
cancer support centre

construction
2008

55. London Design Museum and Holland Green

**224-238 Kensington
High Street**
London W8 6AG

Mon - Sun / 10 am - 6 pm

+44 (0) 20 38625900

designmuseum.org

Circle / District
High Street Kensington

The new London Design Museum was created following the refurbishment of the former Commonwealth Institute, a Modernist building designed by Robert Matthew Johnson-Marshall & Partners in 1962, renowned for its distinctive parabolic copper roof, visible both internally and externally.

The renovation project was designed by OMA and Allies & Morrison, with interior layout by John Pawson. It involved the restoration of the pre-existing Grade II listed building, and the creation of exhibition areas, teaching workshops, an auditorium, a restaurant and a bookshop. The end result is a 10 thousand square metre Design Museum, currently the largest of its kind in the world.

The surrounding area, Holland Green, underwent wide-scale redevelopment, with the creation of green parks and pedestrian walks designed by landscape architects, West 8. Close to the museum are three apartment buildings; identical stone cubes, but of different sizes, whose façades feature regular rows of tall narrow windows, interrupted in certain points by terraces, wide openings, and projecting limestone balconies.

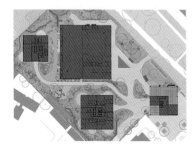

© Nick Guttridge

architects
OMA, Allies and Morrison,
John Pawson, West 8

type
museum, public space,
residential

construction
2016

56. One Kensington Gardens

8 Kensington Road
London W8 5PE

external viewing only

Circle / District
High Street Kensington

This new residential complex, completed in 2015 and designed by David Chipperfield Architects, has a beautiful location facing Kensington Gardens. It hosts 97 prestigious apartments, each one different from the others. The project was to realize three new buildings and reuse the façades of a nineteenth-century terrace incorporated along the fronts giving onto Victoria Road and De Vere Gardens.

All the aspects, except the brick one overlooking the narrower Canning Passage, feature the use of Portland stone. However, they all vary slightly, creating overall harmony while at the same time giving each one its own character. The Kensington Road façade is marked by the strong horizontal lines of the balconies and the bronze parapets that wind a few metres round into the two side streets. Here the rhythm changes and the openings become more regular. Inside the site are internal courtyards which give all of the apartments a great deal of light.

© David Chipperfield Architects

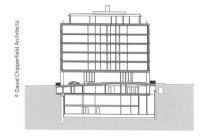

architects
David Chipperfield Architects

type
residential

construction
2015

57. Victoria and Albert Museum / Exhibition Road Quarter

Cromwell Road / Exhibition Road
London SW7 2RL

Sat - Thu / 10 am - 5.45 pm
Fri / 10 am - 10 pm

+44 (0) 20 79422000

www.vam.ac.uk

Circle / District /
Piccadilly
South Kensington

Founded as the Museum of Manufactures in 1852, the Victoria and Albert presently hosts a vast collection of decorative arts in the world. The building that houses it was designed between 1857 and 1909 by Francis Fawke and Aston Webb, who are to thank for the richly eclectic façade. Other features are the magnificent ceramic floors in the interior, the painted vault ceilings and the frescoes by Leighton Corridor.

The Exhibition Road Quarter, designed by AL_A and completed June 2017, transformed a former boiler house looking onto an important London cultural artery, Exhibition Road. Hence, a series of spaces were created which redefine the relationship between the museum and the road. The courtyard, now a new porcelain-covered public space with 11,000 handmade tiles inspired by the museum's rich ceramics collection, was imagined as a new opportunity for the city, a place that can host installations, events and above all which the public can make its own. The courtyard gives onto the Blavatnik Hall, a new entrance to the Museum and leads to the large Sainsbury Gallery.

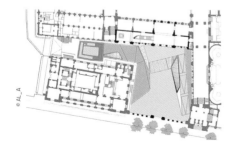

© AL_A

© Hufton+Crow

architects
Francis Fowke / Henry Young
Darracott Scott / Aston Webb
/ AL_A

type
museum

construction
1857 / 1873 / 1909 / 2017

58. One Hyde Park

100 Knightsbridge
London SW1X 7LJ

external viewing only

Piccadilly
Knightsbridge

The new One Hyde Park complex, designed by Rogers Stirk Harbour + Partners in 2005, has contributed to the residential development of the whole area, by linking Knightsbridge back up to Hyde Park. The building comprises 86 apartments and duplexes, including four penthouses and three retail areas on the ground floor along Knightsbridge. Furthermore, there are common areas such as a cinema, a 21-metre swimming pool, squash courts and conference rooms.

The building achieves a top energy performance thanks to its great outer insulating layer. The prestressed concrete structure is visible every two floors on the exterior. On the residential floors, the façade features a series of vertical blades in pre-coated copper alloy, framed by a visible structural framework. The choice of copper is clearly determined by the desire to dialogue with the colours and textures of the surrounding red-brick buildings.

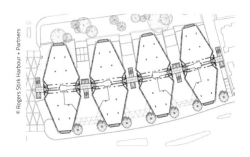

© Rogers Stirk Harbour + Partners

architects
Rogers Stirk Harbour +
Partners

type
residential

construction
2011

59. Serpentine Sakler Gallery

W Carriage Drive
London W2 2AR

open to the public only
during exhibitions
Tue - Sat / 10 am - 6 pm

+44 (0) 20 74026075
information@
serpentinegalleries.org
www.serpentinegalleries.org

Central
Lancaster Gate

The project sets out to restructure and expand the original building, an ex-gunpowder
store in Kensington Gardens dating from the
Napoleonic wars.

The building, which hosts a sequence of exhibition spaces a bit like Russian dolls, displays great care for detail. A new covered
square, created by closing and cladding the
old courtyards, acts as a rest area, while
the interior rooms, with no natural light, are
only used for performances, audio and video
works, and sculpture.

A corridor links the main exhibition space
to the adjacent restaurant where you find
yourself under the waves of a sort of para-
chute, a glass-fibre fabric membrane ceiling with three layers of insulation, covered
in polytetrafluoroethylene (PTFE). The roof
of the Sackler Gallery, stretched between a
perimetral ring and five processed steel pillars, bears the obvious stamp of Zaha Hadid:
unmistakeable composite curves, smoothly
integrated into an unbroken surface which
at certain points swells and brushes against
the ground and at others laps against the
glass-free walls.

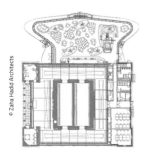

© Zaha Hadid Architects

© Luke Hayes

architects
Zaha Hadid Architects

type
exhibition centre

construction
2013

60. Paddington Station

Praed Street
London W2 1HQ

open to the public

+44 345 711 4141

networkrail.co.uk

 Circle / Hammersmith
& City / Bakerloo /
District
Paddington Station

The first building at Paddington Station was a temporary structure with a wooden roof made following the design of Isambard Kingdom Brunel. First coming into operation in 1838, it had just four platforms. Just a few years later, in 1854, with the increase in rail traffic, Brunel was again commissioned with the project to extend and build a new roof for the station. This also involved the architect Matthew Digby Wyatt, secretary of the Royal Commission for the Great Exhibition, and businessmen Fox and Henderson, who both took part in realizing the Crystal Palace project, from which the new Paddington Station drew inspiration.

The three vaulted ceilings are composed of wrought iron ribs which support the curved glass and rest on three rows of slender cast iron columns. The station was expanded again at the beginning of the 20th century with a fourth arch parallel to the three existing ones, while in the second half of the century, the covering and glass panels were replaced by elements faithful to the originals. Since the 1990s, further operations have been underway to restore, consolidate and modernize the structure.

architects	type	construction
Isambard Kingdom Brunel	railway station	1838

61. Paddington Green Campus at City of Westminster College

Paddington Green
London W2 1NB

partly open to the public

+44 (0) 20 77238826
international@cwc.ac.uk
www.cwc.ac.uk

 Bakerloo
Edgware Road

The college is built on the site of an existing building at Paddington Green, in a delicate urban context. The simple and essential geometric shapes of the building revolve around a large central atrium, giving the interior spaces a flexible layout. Light-filled and clad with light-coloured wooden panels alternating with concrete elements, the hall reinforces the dialogue between interior and exterior and provides students with a common area where they can interact.

The east and west façades of the building are clad with protective translucent, full-height 'fins'. The south side is shaded by a big overhang and a large translucent roof made of ethylene tetrafluoroethylene (ETFE), a special transparent plastic material, closes off the atrium, guaranteeing insulation and natural light.

Situated close to the main entrance of the building are areas for socialisation and free time, amongst which a theatre, exhibition gallery and coffee shop.

© Schmidt Hammer Lassen Architects

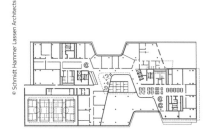

© Adam Mørk

architects
Schmidt Hammer Lassen
Architects

type
campus

construction
2010

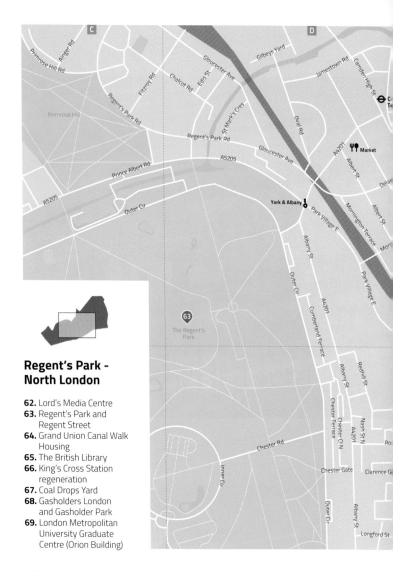

Regent's Park - North London

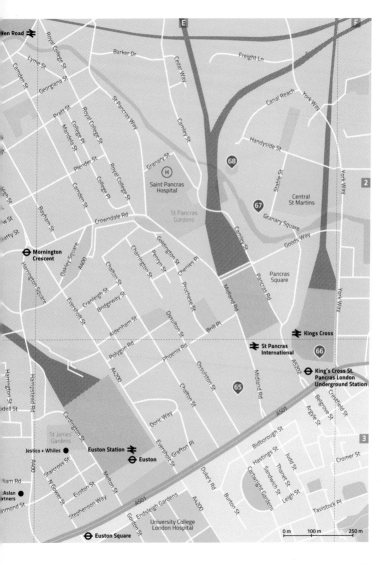

62. Lord's Media Centre

St John's Wood Road
London NW8 8QN

open to the public only during
specific events

+44 (0) 20 76168501
events@lords.org
www.lords.org

 Jubilee
St John's Wood

The Lord's Cricket Ground Media Centre rises up over the stands. Capable of hosting over 100 journalists on the lower floor, the upper floor contains the television and radio commentators' boxes.

Held up exclusively by the structures inside the two lift shafts and stairways, the Lord's Media Centre is one of London's most innovative buildings, both thanks to its aerodynamic shape and the building techniques used. The building was constructed following the most recent shipbuilding technology. The casing, made completely of aluminium, is a smooth white shell, while the side facing the ground is a large, unbroken window which is slanted to avoid reflections, so that journalists from all over the world can follow and commentate all the phases of the game as comfortably as possible.

© Future Systems

architects
Future Systems

type
media centre

construction
1999

63. Regent's Park and Regent Street

Regent's Park, Regent Street

open to the public

Bakerloo
Regent's Park

The project came about from the desire to build a residential area around Marylebone Park, later renamed Regent's Park, and to connect it to St James's Park by a new road, called Regent Street. The undertaking by John Nash resulted in the greatest reorganization of architecture and town layout in the whole of 19th-century England.

Both the neighbourhood and the road are made of long rows of terraced houses, according to the principle that streets are not formed by a series of single buildings side by side, but by edifices designed as a single organism. Both the terraced houses and the semicircular Park Crescent which links the park and Regent Street clearly derive from the Bath townhouses by John Wood father and son.

Nash moulded all the new buildings in a clearly Neoclassical style, with ample use of porticoes with arches on pillars, columns, beams and tympanums. A further classical feature is the employment of white plaster and stucco in a city that then, as now, was dominated by exposed brickwork.

architects
John Nash

type
residential,
public space

construction
1811 - 1825

64. Grand Union Canal Walk Housing

Hawley Crescent
London NW1 8NP

external viewing only

 Northern
Camden Town

When he was assigned to design some homes as part of a commission for a Sainsbury's supermarket in Camden, it was Grimshaw himself who proposed creating separate houses rather than a single apartment block.

The earmarked site, a narrow sliver of land along the canal, decided the conformation of the strip of terraced houses (which consists of ten three-bedroom homes, one one-bedroom maisonette and a bedsit), as well as the interior layout of the flats, which feature white plaster walls and beech wood stairs, floors and other details, in contrast with the hi-tech materials used for the exterior. The south-facing walls have no windows, while the walls overlooking the canal display unusual circular windows creating openings in the metal fronts.

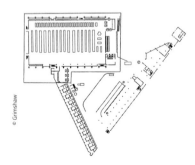

© Grimshaw

architects
Grimshaw

type
residential

construction
1988

65. The British Library

96 Euston Road
London NW1 2DB

Mon, Wed, Thu, Fri /
9.30 am - 6 pm
Tue / 9.30 am - 8 pm
Sat / 9.30 am - 5 pm
Sun / 11 am - 5 pm

+44 (0) 20 74127332
visitor-services@bl.uk
www.bl.uk

Circle / Hammersmith
& City / Metropolitan
/ Northern / Piccadilly
/ Victoria
King's Cross St Pancras

Amongst political clashes, financial problems and bureaucratic issues, Colin St John Wilson took almost 40 years to see his design for the British Library, the most important and biggest public work done in London in the last quarter of the twentieth century, come to light.

Initially, in 1962, a site in Bloomsbury, close to the British Museum, had been singled out for the building. But the library was eventually concluded in 1997 in an area further north, situated between Euston and St Pancras stations.

With its deliberately anti-monumental appearance, the large and intricate building, organised around a vast square, evidently draws from Aalto and Asplund's civic building projects. The inside of the building is laid out in an eminently functional manner, with great care for detail. Situated in the centre is a six-floor glass tower containing the King's Library, with the 65,000 printed volumes, plus pamphlets, manuscripts and maps, collected by King George III between 1763 and 1820.

architects
Colin St John Wilson
and Partners

type
library

construction
1997

66. King's Cross Station regeneration

Euston Road
London N1 9AP

open to the public

+44 (0) 20 34791795

www.kingscross.co.uk

**Circle / Hammersmith
& City / Metropolitan
/ Northern / Piccadilly
/ Victoria**
King's Cross St Pancras

Completed on occasion of the 2012 Olympics, the regeneration of King's Cross Station has strengthened its image as one of the city's architectural icons, combining reuse, restoration and new construction. The project pointed the station in a new west-facing direction, creating significant improvements from a logistical point of view, and highlighting the main façade of the original station from 1852 by Lewis Cubitt.

The netted structure of the semicircular ceiling, held up by 16 columns which branch out towards the sky like trees, multiplies the size of the space compared to the existing station. The structure, consisting of a single mesh of steel tubes, rises up to around 20 metres from ground level and covers a surface area of 7,500 square metres.

The three floors of the original building have been restored and a shopping gallery built around the outside. The master plan for the new station also proved an influence on the infrastructure of the urban fabric, making it a driving force in regenerating the surrounding urban context.

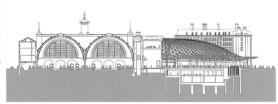

© John Mc Aslan + Partners

architects
John McAslan + Partners /
Stanton Williams

type
railway station

construction
2012

67. Coal Drops Yard

11 Stable St, King's Cross
London N1C 4AB

open to the public

+44 (0) 20 79402900
coaldropsyard@anmcomms.
com
www.coaldropsyard.com

**Circle / Hammersmith
& City / Metropolitan
/ Northern / Piccadilly
/ Victoria**
King's Cross St Pancras

This ambitious intervention, commissioned in 2014 by the King's Cross Development Partnership, was achieved in a very short time. It involved the transformation of a Victorian railway yard, built around 1850 in the King's Cross area, to create a modern shopping district through a refined operation of urban regeneration. The two heritage buildings, originally constructed for the unloading and storage of coal from the north of England, now house 55 retail stores of various sizes connected to each other by a series of cleverly designed walkways, bridges and stairs.

The main feature of the project is the sinuous roof design that begins from the gabled roofs of each edifice, extending like curved bands over the central area between the buildings until they make contact with each other, creating a new suspended upper story with a completely glazed façade, and below, a partially covered public space that welcomes visitors, drawing them into the complex.

This clever solution was able to restore two historical buildings, combining them, using advanced structural technology in a modern design with strong visual impact.

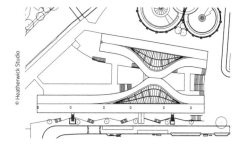

© Heatherwick Studio

© Hutton+Crow

architects	type	construction
Heatherwick Studio	market	2018

68. Gasholders London and Gasholder Park

14-15 Stable Street
London N1C 4AB

open to the public

+44 (0) 98 07464022
enquiries@gasholderslondon.
co.uk
gasholderslondon.co.uk

**Circle / Hammersmith
& City / Metropolitan
/ Northern / Piccadilly
/ Victoria**
King's Cross St Pancras

Gasholders London is an innovative project which repurposes three cast iron gas holder frames dating back to 1867. The gas holders were abandoned after plans began for the re-development of the ex-industrial Kings Cross area. The cylindrical buildings constructed inside the frames are of different heights, re-calling the rise and fall of historic gasometers according to the quantity of gas contained. Externally, the structures maintain their original industrial features, while the internal spaces have a light dynamic design thanks to the play of curved staircases and circular balcony walkways. The external structural cladding is composed of vertical modular steel and glass panels that also provide shade and privacy inside the apartments.

At the intersection of the three frames is a circular open courtyard that forms the core of the complex and an atrium for the buildings that house 145 apartments designed by the Jonathan Tuckey Design, as well a series of private facilities, including a gym, spa, business lounge and screening room.

Adjacent to the three gasometer buildings is a fourth, called Gasholder Park, which has been transformed into an urban green park by Bell Phillips Architects.

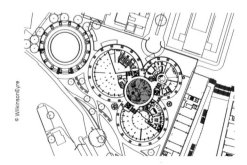

© WilkinsonEyre

© Peter Landers

architects
WilkinsonEyre,
Bell Phillips Architects

type
residential, public space

construction
2018

69. London Metropolitan University Graduate Centre (Orion Building)

166-220 Holloway Road
London N7 8DB

Mon - Fri / 8 am - 9 pm
Sat / 8 am - 3 pm

+44 (0) 20 71332072

www.londonmet.ac.uk

 Piccadilly
Holloway Road

Libeskind's first project in London, this small university building with its remarkable architectural impact and strong interior-exterior relations slots into quite an anonymous part of north London. It is a sparkling sculpture of three volumes of reflective steel slashed by irregular window openings which point in different directions and overlap. The composition is in line with the US architect's typical language, despite the quite limited budget compared to his usual commissions.

The new building's interior, with its variously sloping white plaster walls, hosts some classrooms, a 100-seater main hall, and a series of links with the different wings making up the Metropolitan University. The lighting elements are fixed on steel tracks that etch the ceilings and create the night-time image of the whole building.

© Studio Libeskind

© Eiffel Brecht

architects
Studio Libeskind

type
university premises

construction
2004

Docklands -
Olympic Park -
East End

70. Rivington Place
71. Adelaide Wharf
72. QMUL Graduate Centre
73. Westfield Student Village
74. Aquatics Centre
75. Velodrome
76. The Stratford

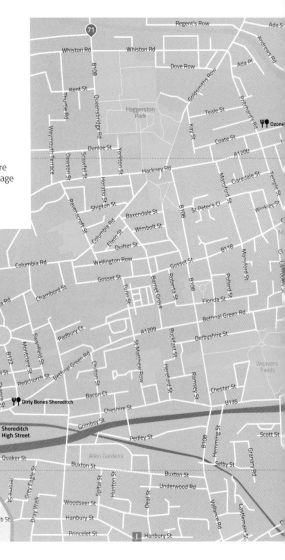

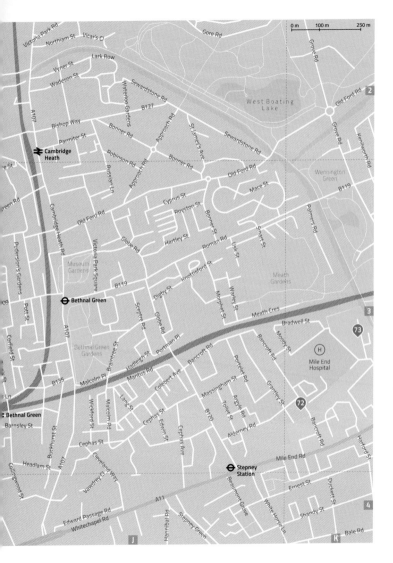

Victoria Park Rd
Northiam St
Vicar's Cl
Gore Rd
Grove Rd
Lark Row
Vyner St
Wadeson St
Seward stone Rd
B127
Waterloo Gardens
West Boating Lake
Old Ford Rd
2
Bishop Way
Bonner Rd
Approach Rd
St James's Ave
Sewardstone Rd
Grove Rd
Kenworthy Rd
Parmiter St
≷ Cambridge Heath
Robinson Rd
Bonner Rd
Old Ford Rd
Mace St
Wennington Green
B119
A107
Russian Ln
Approach Rd
Cyprus St
Royston St
Bonner St
Palmers Rd
Green Rd
Cambridge Heath Rd
Old Ford Rd
Globe Rd
Hartley St
Roman Rd
Usk St
Smart St
Pudersjon's Gardens
Museum Gardens
Victoria Park Square
B119
Knottisford St
Digby St
Wapley St
Morpeth St
Moach Gardens
Port St
⊖ Bethnal Green
Sceptre Rd
Globe Rd
Meath Cres
Bradwell St
3
Corfield St
A107
Bethnal Green Gardens
Braintree St
Hadleigh St
Portman Pl
Bancroft Rd
Mostyn St
73
H
Mile End Hospital
B135
Malcolm Pl
Mantus Rd
Colebert Ave
Bancroft St
Portelet Rd
Gransley St
⫴ Bethnal Green
Wickford St
Malcolm Rd
Lant St
Cephas St
Edwin St
Massingham St
Argyle Rd
Troilet St
B120
Bancroft Rd
72
Harford St
Barnsley St
Brickhurst St
Cephas St
Cleveland Way
Cephas Ave
Alderney Rd
Mile End Rd
Ernest St
Durkett St
Headlam St
A107
⊖ Stepney Station
Beaumont Grove
White Horse Ln
Shandy St
4
Collingwood St
Vawdrey Cl
A11
Edward Passage Rd
Whitechapel Rd
Hanbury Rd
Stepney Green
Bale Rd
J
K

4

E India Dock Rd
A1020

80

Coriander Ave.
Nutmeg Ln
Saffron Ave.
Oregano Dr.
E India Dock Rd

Brunel St
Turner St
Jude St

Silvocea Way
Limmo
Peninsula
Ecological
Park

Holt St
Peto St N
Caxton St N

Lower Lear Lea Crossing

Lower Lea Crossing

Naval Row
Aspen Way

Newport Ave.
Pilgrims Mews
Jamestone Way

Orchard Pl.

5

Paul Julius Cl

Blackwall Tunnel South

A 102

46
The O2

Waterview Dr
Meridian Gate
Tunnel Ave

47

48 Cutter Ln

Thames

⊖ **North Greenwich**
Station

Phoenix Ave

Green Pl.

6

Thames

A102

Tunnel Ave

Edmund Halley Way

W Parkside

E Parkside

Millennium Way

Pilot Walk
Barge Walk
Bessemer

M

N

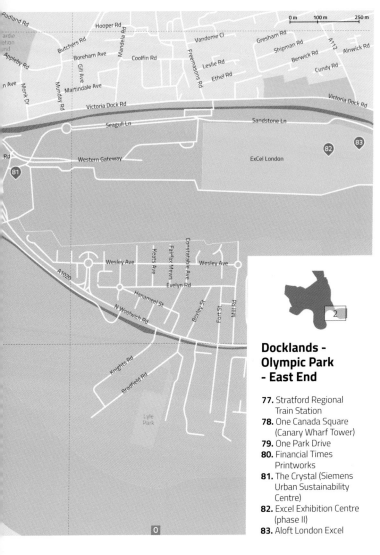

0 m   100 m   250 m

Radland Rd

Hooper Rd

Vandome Cl

Gresham Rd

Shipman Rd

A112

Alnwick Rd

Berwick Rd

ardie
ation
und

Appleby Rd

Butchers Rd

Mandela Rd

Boreham Ave

Coolfin Rd

Freemasons Rd

Leslie Rd

Cundy Rd

Gill Ave

Ethel Rd

n Ave

Monk Dr

Munday Rd

Martindale Ave

Victoria Dock Rd

Victoria Dock Rd

Seagull Ln

Sandstone Ln

Rd

Western Gateway

ExCel London

82

83

81

Constable Ave

Fairfax Mews

Keats Ave

A1020

Wesley Ave

Wesley Ave

Evelyn Rd

Hanameel St

Baxter St

Fort St

Mill Rd

N Woolwich Rd

Knights Rd

Bradfield Rd

Lyle
Park

0

2

Docklands -
Olympic Park
- East End

77. Stratford Regional
    Train Station
78. One Canada Square
    (Canary Wharf Tower)
79. One Park Drive
80. Financial Times
    Printworks
81. The Crystal (Siemens
    Urban Sustainability
    Centre)
82. Excel Exhibition Centre
    (phase II)
83. Aloft London Excel

70. Rivington Place

**Rivington Street,
Rivington Place**
London EC2A 3BA

Tue, Wed, Fri / 11 am - 6 pm
Thu / 11 am - 9 pm
Sat / 12 am - 6 pm

+44 (0) 20 77491240
info@rivingtonplace.org
www.rivingtonplace.org

London Overground
Shoreditch High Street

The building, a solid, long rectangular-shaped block on the corner between Rivington Street and Rivington Place, presents singular façades with an irregular rectangular grid surface pattern. The chequered pattern alternates anthracite-coloured concrete blocks with gaps made of glossy black aluminium or glass sheets. The distinctive pitched roof seems to be a reference to the industrial architecture typical of this part of the city.

This stern external appearance is in contrast with the surprisingly bright and welcoming interiors. The approximately 1,500 square metres are distributed through a triple-height atrium encircled by public spaces and access to the upper floors.

The building hosts the administrative offices of the Institute of International Visual Art and Autograph ABP (Association of Black Photographers), two organizations which have been interested in the work of artists from different cultural backgrounds, and in promoting the development and spread of experimentation in the field of the visual arts, for around twenty years.

© Adjaye Associates

architects
Adjaye Associates

type
multi-purpose building

construction
2007

71. Adelaide Wharf

120 Queensbridge Road
London E2 8FB

external viewing only

www.adelaidewharf.com

London Overground
Haggerston

This residential complex, alongside a park and a canal, hosts both social housing and houses on the open market, as well as some offices on the ground floor.

The designers' idea was for a compact, six-storey building, with a U-shaped layout. On the ground floor, the block is 'pierced' at several points to enable access to the picturesque central courtyard with trees.

The façades are characterised by a modular prefabricated casing made of strips of coarsely cut larch wood which brings to mind the old packing chest warehouse that once occupied the site. This results in an undifferentiated façade, whose volumes are marked almost exclusively by singular coloured balconies in various tones of yellow, orange and red.

© Allford Hall Monaghan Morris

architects
Allford Hall Monaghan Morris

type
residential

construction
2007

72. QMUL Graduate Centre

Bancroft Road, Mile End Road
London E1 4DH

partly open to the public
Mon - Fri / 8 am - 6 pm
Sat - Sun / closed

+44 (20) 78825555
admissions@qmul.ac.uk
www.qmul.ac.uk

**District /
Hammersmith & City**
Stepney Green

This new centre, designed by WilkinsonEyre, was the prize-winning project in a competition launched in 2012 to celebrate the 125th anniversary of this prestigious London university. The project also includes outdoor spaces, and has made a significant contribution to urban and landscape improvements in the western part of the campus facing Bancroft Road.

The angled brick building is set on a completely glazed, double level foundation base with striking V-shaped support pillars. The base houses the foyer, a café with a large outdoor social area, study rooms, a 200 seat lecture hall and other seminar rooms. The School of Economics and Finance is spread over the top four floors. On the roof of the building is a floating glass box that contains graduate reading rooms and a common room that opens onto a large outdoor terrace.

© WilkinsonEyre

© Jack Hobhouse

architects
WilkinsonEyre

type
educational spaces

construction
2017

73. Westfield Student Village

Westfield Way
London E1 4PD

external viewing only

**Central / District /
Hammersmith & City**
Mile End

These two buildings, which provide accommodation for 1,200 students, make up the biggest university campus in London. The first, eight-storey block, runs parallel to the railway line close to Liverpool Street Station, while the other lower-rise building faces Mile End Park and the canal.

Both buildings feature the use of copper cladding, in one case coated, and in the other oxidized, and adopt prefabrication techniques.

The detailed layout of the buildings attempts to offer a whole series of spaces with different characteristics and levels of privacy and the maximum possible variety of room types (19 in total), to reduce the typical sameness of student lodgings to a minimum.

A new public square connects the campus with the nearby university buildings.

© Feilden Clegg Bradley Studios

© Feilden Clegg Bradley Studios

architects
Feilden Clegg Bradley Studios

type
residential

construction
2008

74. Aquatics Centre

Queen Elizabeth Olympic Park
London E20 2ZQ

Mon - Sun / 6 am - 10.30 pm

+44 (0) 20 85363150
customerservices@
queenelizabetholympicpark.co.uk
www.queenelizabetholympicpark.
co.uk

**Central / London
Overground / DLR**
Stratford

The design of the Aquatics Centre was inspired by the fluid dynamics of water in motion, clearly visible in the undulating roof that sweeps upwards like a rising wave to enclose the centre pool in a single curve, sloping downwards until it meets the Stratford City pedestrian bridge. The fluid shape continues inside the building with the design for the diving pool platform areas.

The configuration of the curving roof, anchored in the ground in three points, made it possible to install 7,500 additional temporary seats for 15,000 spectators along both sides of the building during the Olympic Games. Following the games, the extra seating stands were removed and replaced with glass panels, maintaining 2,500 seats for spectators.

Opposite, on the other side of the Waterworks River, are the new Olympic Stadium designed by the Populous architectural firm, and the iconic ArcelorMittal Orbit, the urban sculpture created for the Olympics by Anish Kapoor and Cecil Balmond: a mainly recycled steel lattice mesh structure, composed of 9 kms of tubular profiles, 1,800 connecting plates, and 900 steel joint nodes.

© Zaha Hadid Architects

© Hufton+Crow

architects
Zaha Hadid Architects

type
sports centre

construction
2011

75. Velodrome

Queen Elizabeth Olympic Park
London E20 3AB

Mon - Sun / 9 am - 10 pm

+44 (0) 845 6770600
velopark@leevalleypark.org.uk

London Overground
Hackney Wick

The London Velodrome, designed for the 2012 Olympics, is located in the northern part of the Olympic area and can contain up to 6,000 spectators. Unlike other competition venues, it was designed as a permanent building.

The Velodrome is characterised by a saddle-shaped, shell-like roof, with taut steel cables inside the edge truss and a wooden panel finish. The roof, whose curved shape reflects the circuit in the interior, is broken up by eight strips of skylights which reduce the need for artificial light during the day.

The external cover is formed by numerous planks of red cedar, supported by a steel structure. The elevated entrance level follows the circuit round and is entirely glazed, so anyone who moves around during the races can keep the competition in their sight at all times.

© Hopkins Architects Partnership

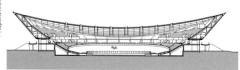

© Nathanie Moore

architects
Hopkins Architects,
Grant Associates

type
sports centre

construction
2011

76. The Stratford

**Queen Elizabeth Olympic Park,
20 International Way**
London E20 1FD

open to the public

+44 (0) 20 39613333
info@thestratford.com
www.thestratford.com

 DLR
Stratford International

Located near one of London's main transport hubs, Stratford International Station, with views over the Olympic Park, this ground-breaking, 42 floor tower houses a boutique hotel and 248 apartments with a large variety of residential typologies that range from flexible studios to double-story penthouses. It also features two restaurants, an exclusive cocktail bar, gym, meeting and conference rooms. Numerous common areas were designed to encourage social interaction among the residents. The triple-height lobby forms a social hub shared by apartment residents and hotel guests.

The tower's complex concrete and steel structure was achieved using powerful cantilevered beams and high-precision load balance calculations, resulting in deep notches cut through the building to create sky gardens on the 7th, 25th, and 36th floors with spectacular views of the city.

Close attention was paid to selecting construction materials, with extensive use of recycled steel and concrete, solar panel energy, and cutting edge control systems for lighting and heat dispersion to guarantee very high environmentally sustainable levels.

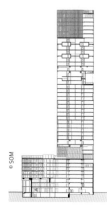

© SOM

Courtesy SOM © Hufton+Crow

architects
SOM

type
hotel, multi-purpose building,
residential

construction
2018

77. Stratford Regional Train Station

Station Street, Stratford
London E15 1AZ

open to the public

 **DLR / Jubilee /
Central / London
Overground**
Stratford

In 1994, WilkinsonEyre was selected to re-develop Stratford Station, situated on the new extension of the Jubilee Line, in the immediate vicinity of what would later become the 2012 Olympic Park. The challenge was to create a new structure combining functionality and good-quality architecture, and to give the new line a precise identity.

The new building, completed five years later, consists of a simple and intriguing curved metal roof with three of its sides seeming to rest on the glass walls. Underneath, it creates a single large covered area, with a completely different layout to the existing station. The roof also allows natural ventilation and a 'chimney effect' which leads to perfect regulation of the heat in the main station hall.

© WilkinsonEyre

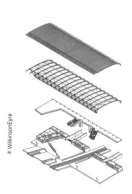

architects
WilkinsonEyre /
JLEP architects

type
railway station

construction
1999

78. One Canada Square (Canary Wharf Tower)

1 Canada Square
London E14 5AB

partly open to the public

 Jubilee / DLR
Canary Wharf

Also known as Canary Wharf Tower, with its 50 floors spanning almost 250 metres in height, it was the city's tallest skyscraper until July 2012, when it was overtaken by Renzo Piano's The Shard.

The tall, basic parallelepiped clad in steel and glass is crowned by a distinctive pyramidal roof, which immediately made it a symbol of contemporary London.

The construction of this building paved the way for the Canary Wharf complex which today hosts some of the city's tallest and most representative skyscrapers, amongst which Norman Foster's HSBC Tower, completed in 2002, and the two Citigroup buildings, one designed by Pelli and the other again by Foster, finished between 1999 and 2001.

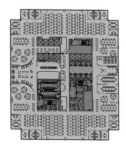

architects
Pelli Clarke Pelli Architects

type
offices, retail

construction
1991

79. One Park Drive

1 Park Drive
London E14 5JJ

external viewing only

+44 (0) 20 7001 3800
residential.sales@
canarywharf.com
residential.canarywharf.com/
one-park-drive

 Jubilee / DLR
Canary Wharf

This new cylindrical, 58 storey, residential tower is located at Canary Wharf, and will be completed at the end of 2020. It is part of the wider master plan to redefine one of the last remaining areas of the former docklands that has not yet been redeveloped.

Varying shapes and depth of balconies and terraces create an irregular configuration; alternating recessed and projecting elements, and solid and glazed sections, identify the different types of apartment in the overall design. The 483 apartments, with interior design by Bowler James Brindley, all enjoy generous views over South Dock and the city. There are three types of accommodation: the lowest part of the tower contains loft-style apartments with high ceilings and substantial outdoor space. The central section houses the smaller apartments called "clusters", and the top section contains the largest sky loft apartments. Private facilities for residents include a lobby and concierge service, library, screening room, and health and fitness suite.

© Herzog & de Meuron

architects
Herzog & de Meuron

type
residential

construction
2020

80. Financial Times Printworks

240 East India Dock Road
London E14 9YY

external viewing only

DLR
East India

This large building, designed by Nicholas Grimshaw to house the printworks of one of the most renowned newspapers in Europe, was made in 1988 in just 12 months. Right from the start it became an immediately recognisable landmark for those coming into London from the east. These days it has been converted to host the London Data Centre.

The architect imagined a flexible and open layout, divided into two clearly distinct wings, separated by a central body with two service towers. The rooms designed to host the print machines, enclosed by a surface of 96-metre long structural glass panes, are completely visible from the outside. The remaining parts of the building are clad with special aluminium panels devised especially for this project.

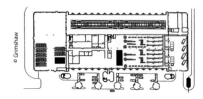

© Grimshaw

architects
Grimshaw

type
industrial, offices

construction
1988

81. The Crystal (Siemens Urban Sustainability Centre)

**One Siemens Brothers Way,
Royal Victoria Dock**
London E16 1GB

Tue - Fri / 10 am - 5 pm
Sat - Sun / 10 am - 7 pm

+44 (0) 20 70556400
info@thecrystal.org
www.thecrystal.org

 DLR
Royal Victoria

The Crystal is situated in east London, at the end of the Royal Victoria Docks, on the opposite side of the Thames to the Millennium Dome. It is an area that is experiencing a big property boom, with the regeneration of the historic docks creating an important advanced technological district.

The multidisciplinary hub is designed around the themes of urban sustainability and features façades made of glass panels which are tilted in such a way as to make optimum use of the sunlight. Inside, the surface area of around 2,000 square metres hosts a 270-seater conference hall, a restaurant and it welcomes over 100,000 visitors a year.

The building has been built in observance of the strictest environmental standards; it uses solar energy, low-energy geothermal heat pumps, LED lighting and rainwater collection, and no fossil fuels.

© WilkinsonEyre

architects
WilkinsonEyre

type
offices, exhibition centre,
conference hall

construction
2010

82. Excel Exhibition Centre (phase II)

One Western Gateway, Royal Victoria Dock
London E16 1XL

open to the public only during specific events

+44 (0) 20 70695000
info@excel-london.co.uk
www.excel-london.co.uk

DLR
Custom House

The operation consists of an extension to the first lot of the Excel Exhibition Centre, a trade fair centre made in 2001 according to the design of Moxley Architects, whose regular layout consisted of a central corridor with exhibition pavilions on both sides, and access from the side to load and unload goods.

The Phase II project has created a large entrance, giving the complex a strong identity and a new place in the urban setting. The spiral on the façade, covered in yellow polyester, marks the eastern entrance to the exhibition space and continues inside as an extruded volume suspended on sloping steel pillars. This creates a covered passage overlooked by cafés, restaurants, conference rooms and multi-purpose spaces at the service of the exhibition areas. From the structural point of view, the new, 15-metre-plus-tall block has the appearance of a single-span megastructure obtained with the use of serial modules, and it is made with particular attention to thermal comfort and saving energy.

© Grimshaw

architects	type	construction
Grimshaw	exhibition centre, multi-purpose centre	2000 / 2010

83. Aloft London Excel

**One Eastern Gateway,
Royal Victoria Dock**
London E16 1FR

partly open to the public

+44 (0) 20 32030700
aloftlondonexcel@
reservestarwood.com
www.aloftlondonexcel.com

DLR
Prince Regent

The Aloft London Excel is a new top hotel situated in the ExCeL campus in the London Docklands area. The project was developed by ExCeL's parent organisation, the Abu Dhabi National Exhibitions Company, in collaboration with Starwood Hotels & Resorts Worldwide.

The building is laid out in a long, sinewy shape, with a central backbone containing rooms and access to the upper floors, with two concave side wings alongside hosting additional rooms and corridors. These wings are clad with thousands of highly reflective stainless steel tiles which create an extraordinary chromatic effects, changing colour throughout the day. The central backbone of the hotel is finished with double-glazed cladding whose horizontal stripes give the building more movement.

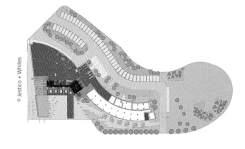

© Jestico + Whiles

© Tim Crocker

architects	**type**	**construction**
Jestico + Whiles	hotel	2011

Museums

Apsley House / Wellington Museum
Museum dedicated to the Duke of Wellington
-
149 Piccadilly, London W1

www.english-heritage.org.uk/daysout/
properties/apsley-house
-
Tel +44 (0) 20 7499 5676

Banqueting House
Historic museum
-
Whitehall, London, SW1A 2ER

www.hrp.org.uk/banqueting-house
BanquetingHouse@hrp.org.uk
Tel +44 (0) 20 3166 6000

The British Museum
Museum of cultural history and civilisations
-
Great Russel Street, London WC1

www.britishmuseum.org
information@britishmuseum.org
Tel +44 (0) 20 7323 8299

Buckingham Palace
Royal palace
-
Buckingham Gate, London SW1A 1AA

www.royal.uk/royal-residences-buckingham-
palace
-
-

Geffrye Museum
Museum of the home
-
136 Kingsland Road, London E2

www.geffrye-museum.org.uk
info@geffrye-museum.org.uk
Tel +44 (0) 20 7739 9893

Houses of Parliament (Palace of Westminster)
Seat of Parliament
-
Westminster, London SW1A 0AA

www.parliament.uk
-
Tel +44 (0) 20 7219 4114

Imperial War Museum
War museum
-
Lambeth Road, London SE1

www.iwm.org.uk
mail@iwm.org.uk
Tel +44 (0) 20 7416 5000

London Design Museum
Design museum
-
224-238 Kensington High Street,
London W8 6AG

designmuseum.org
-
Tel +44 (0) 20 3862 5900

Madame Tussauds
Waxworks museum
-
Marylebone Road, London NW1

www.madame-tussauds.com/london
guest.experience@madame-tussauds.com
Tel +44 (0) 871 894 3000

Museum of London
London history museum
-
150 London Wall, London EC2

www.museumoflondon.org.uk
info@museumoflondon.org.uk
Tel +44 (0) 20 7001 9844

Museum of London Docklands
History of the Thames museum
-
No.1 Warehouse, W India Dock Rd, London
E14

www.museumoflondon.org.uk/docklands
info.docklands@museumoflondon.org.uk
Tel +44 (0) 20 7001 9844

National Gallery
Art gallery
-
Trafalgar Square, London WC2

www.nationalgallery.org.uk
information@ng-london.org.uk
Tel +44 (0) 20 7747 2885

National Maritime Museum
Maritime museum
-
Romney Road, Greenwich, London SE10

www.rmg.co.uk/national-maritime-museum
-
Tel +44 (0) 20 8858 4422

National Portrait Gallery
European portrait museum
-
St Martin's Place, London WC2

www.npg.org.uk
-
Tel +44 (0) 20 7306 0055

Natural History Museum
Natural history museum
-
Cromwell Road, London SW7

www.nhm.ac.uk
-
Tel +44 (0) 20 7942 5000

Science Museum
Science museum
-
Exhibition Road, London SW7

www.sciencemuseum.org.uk
info@sciencemuseum.ac.uk
Tel +44 (0) 870 870 4868

Sir John Soane's Museum
Museum dedicated to John Soane
-
13 Lincoln's Inn Fields, London WC2

www.soane.org
admin@soane.org.uk
Tel +44 (0) 20 7405 2107

Somerset House
Arts museum and centre
-
Strand, London WC2R 1LA

www.somersethouse.org.uk
visitor@somersethouse.org.uk
Tel +44 (0) 20 7845 4600

Tate Britain
Museum of ancient and modern British art
-
Millbank, London SW1

www.tate.org.uk
visiting.britain@tate.org.uk
Tel +44 (0) 20 7887 8888

Tate Modern
Museum of contemporary art
-
Bankside, London SE1

www.tate.org.uk
visiting.modern@tate.org.uk
Tel +44 (0) 20 7887 8888

Tower Bridge
Drawbridge / viewpoint
-
Tower Bridge Road, London SE1 2UP

www.towerbridge.org.uk
enquiries@towerbridge.org.uk
Tel +44 (0) 20 7403 3761

Tower of London
Historic museum
-
Tower Hill, London EC3

www.hrp.org.uk/toweroflondon
visitorservices.tol@hrp.org.uk
Tel +44 (0) 20 3166 6000

Victoria and Albert Museum
Museum of decorative arts
-
Cromwell Road, London SW7

www.vam.ac.uk
vanda@vam.ac.uk
Tel +44 (0) 20 7942 2000

Wallace Collection
Museum of 17th- and 18th-century art
-
Hertford House, Manchester Square,
London W1

www.wallacecollection.org
-
Tel +44 (0) 207 563 9500

Whitechapel Gallery
Museum of modern art
-
77-82 Whitechapel High Street, London E1

www.whitechapelgallery.org
info@whitechapelgallery.org
Tel +44 (0) 20 7522 7888

Theatres

Arcola Theatre
-
24 Ashwin Street, London E8 3DL

www.arcolatheatre.com
boxoffice@arcolatheatre.com
Tel +44 (0) 20 7503 1646

Barbican
-
Silk Street, London EC2Y 8DS

www.barbican.org.uk
tickets@barbican.org.uk
Tel +44 (0) 845 121 6823

Bush Theatre
-
7 Uxbridge Road, London W12 8LJ

www.bushtheatre.co.uk
info@bushtheatre.co.uk
Tel +44 (0) 20 8743 5050

Cadogan Hall
-
5 Sloane Terrace, London SW1X 9DQ

www.cadoganhall.com
-
Tel +44 (0) 20 7730 4500

Donmar Warehouse
-
41 Earlham Street, London WC2H 9LX

www.donmarwarehouse.com
-
Tel +44 (0) 844 871 7624

London Coliseum (English National Opera)
-
St. Martin's Lane, London WC2N 4ES

www.eno.org
box.office@eno.org
Tel +44 (0) 20 7845 9300

National Theatre
-
South Bank, London SE1 9PX

www.nationaltheatre.org.uk
boxoffice@nationaltheatre.org.uk
Tel +44 (0) 20 7452 3000

Old Vic
-
The Cut, London SE1 8NB

www.oldvictheatre.com
-
Tel +44 (0) 844 871 7628

Royal Albert Hall
-
Kensington Gore, London SW7 2AP

www.royalalberthall.com
-
Tel +44 (0) 20 7589 8212

Royal Court Theatre
-
Sloane Square, London SW1W 8AS

www.royalcourttheatre.com
boxoffice@royalcourttheatre.com
Tel +44 (0) 20 7565 5000

Royal Opera House
-
Bow Street, London WC2E 9DD

www.roh.org.uk
-
Tel +44 (0) 20 7304 4000

Shakespeare's Globe
-
21 New Globe Walk, Bankside, London
SE1 9DT

www.shakespearesglobe.com
info@shakespearesglobe.com
Tel +44 (0) 20 7401 9919

Southbank Centre
-
Belvedere Road, London SE1 8XX

www.southbankcentre.co.uk
customer@southbankcentre.co.uk
Tel +44 (0) 20 7960 4200

Wigmore Hall
-
36 Wigmore Street, London W1U 2BP

www.wigmore-hall.org.uk
boxoffice@wigmore-hall.org.uk
Tel +44 (0) 20 7935 2141

Young Vic
-
66 The Cut, London SE1 8LZ

www.youngvic.org
boxoffice@youngvic.org
Tel +44 (0) 20 7922 2922

Restaurants

Aqua Shard
• • •
31 St. Thomas Street, Level 31 The Shard,
London SE1 9RY

www.aquashard.co.uk
aquashardreservations@aqua-london.com
Tel +44 (0) 20 3011 1256

Chez Bruce
• • •
2 Bellevue Road, Wandsworth Common,
London SW17 7EG

www.chezbruce.co.uk
enquiries@chezbruce.co.uk
Tel +44 (0) 20 8672 0114

Fenchurch
• • •
20 Fenchurch Street, Sky garden,
London EC3M 8AF

www.skygarden.london
skygarden@20fenchurchstreet.co.uk
Tel +44 (0) 20 7337 2344

Gaucho Grill
• • •
64 Heat Street, London NW3 1DN

www.gauchorestaurants.co.uk
-
Tel +44 (0) 20 7431 8222

Gordon Ramsay
• • •
68 Royal Hospital Road, London SW3 4HP

www.gordonramsay.com
royalhospitalroad@gordonramsay.com
Tel +44 (0) 20 7352 4441

Medlar
• • •
438 King's Road, London SW10 0LJ

www.medlarrestaurant.co.uk
info@medlarrestaurant.co.uk
Tel +44 (0) 20 7349 1900

St. John
• • •
26 St John Street, London EC1M 4AY

www.stjohnrestaurant.com
reservations@stjohnrestaurant.com
Tel +44 (0) 20 7251 0848

Brasserie Zédel
• •
20 Sherwood Street, London W1F 7ED

www.brasseriezedel.com
reservations@brasseriezedel.com
Tel +44 (0) 20 7734 4888

Coach & Horses
• •
26-28 Ray Street, London EC1R 3DJ

www.thecoachandhorses.com
info@thecoachandhorses.com
Tel +44 (0) 20 7278 8990

Duck & Waffle
• •
Heron Tower, 110 Bishopsgate, London
EC2N 4AY

www.duckandwaffle.com
dwreservations@sushisamba.com
Tel +44 (0) 20 3640 7310

Formans Fish Island
• •
Stour Road, London E3 2NT

www.formans.co.uk
info@formansfishisland.com
Tel +44 (0) 20 8525 2390

Kazan
• •
93-94 Wilton Road, London SW1V 1DW

www.kazan-restaurant.com
kazan.sw1@gmail.com
Tel +44 (0) 20 7233 7100

Kolamba
••
21 Kingly Street, London W1B 5QA

kolamba.co.uk
hello@kolamba.co.uk
Tel +44 (0) 20 3815 4201

••• expensive
•• mid-range
• inexpensive

Launceston Place
••
1A Launceston Place, London W8 5RL

www.launcestonplace-restaurant.co.uk
launcestonplace@danddlondon.com
Tel +44 (0) 20 7937 6912

Moro
••
34-36 Exmouth Market, London EC1R 4QE

www.moro.co.uk
info@moro.co.uk
Tel +44 (0) 20 7833 8336

Ottolenghi
••
287 Upper Street, London N1 2TZ

www.ottolenghi.co.uk
upper@ottolenghi.co.uk
Tel +44 (0) 20 7288 1454

Silo
••
Unit 7 Queens Yard, Hackney Wick,
London E9 5EN

silolondon.com
reservation@silolondon.com
Tel +44 (0) 20 7993 8155

Sketch
••
9 Conduit Street, Mayfair, London W1S 2XG

sketch.london
info@sketch.london
Tel +44 (0) 20 7659 4500

Skylon
••
Royal Festival Hall, Belvedere Road,
London SE1 8XX

www.skylon-restaurant.co.uk
skylonreservations@danddlondon.com
Tel +44 (0) 20 7654 7800

Trullo
••
300-302 Saint Paul's Road, London N1 2LH

www.trullorestaurant.com
enquiries@trullorestaurant.com
Tel +44 (0) 20 7226 2733

Wilder
••
2-4 Boundary Street, Shoreditch,
London E2 7DD

wilderlondon.co.uk
-
Tel +44 (0) 20 7729 1051

Dishoom
•
12 Upper St. Martin's Lane, London
WC2H 9FB

www.dishoom.com
reservations@dishoom.com
Tel +44 (0) 20 7420 9320

Mangal Ocakbasi
•
10 Arcola Street, London E8 2DJ

www.mangal1.com
info@mangal1.com
Tel +44 (0) 20 7275 8981

Ozone Coffee
•
Emma Street, London E2 9AP

ozonecoffee.co.uk
emmastreet@ozonecoffee.co.uk
Tel +44 (0) 20 7490 1039

Hotels

Brown's Hotel
• • •
33 Albemarle Street, London W1S 4BP

www.brownshotel.com
concierge.browns@roccofortehotels.com
Tel +44 (0) 20 7493 6020

Charlotte Street Hotel
• • •
15-17 Charlotte Street, London W1T 1RJ

www.charlottestreethotel.com
charlotte@firmdale.com
Tel +44 (0) 20 7806 2000

Claridge's
• • •
49 Brook Street, London W1K 4HR

www.claridges.co.uk
info@claridges.co.uk
Tel +44 (0) 20 7629 8860

Dorset Square Hotel
• • •
39-40 Dorset Square, London NW1 6QN

www.firmdalehotels.com
dorset@firmdale.com
Tel +44 (0) 20 7723 7874

Nobu Hotel Shoreditch
• • •
10-50 Willow Street, London EC2A 4BH

www.nobuhotels.com
stay-shoreditch@nobuhotels.com
Tel +44 (0) 20 7683 1200

One Aldwych
• • •
1 Aldwych, London WC2B 4BZ

www.onealdwych.co.uk
reservations@onealdwych.com
Tel +44 (0) 20 7300 1000

The Goring
• • •
15 Beeston Place, London SW1W 0JW

www.thegoring.com
reception@thegoring.com
Tel +44 (0) 20 7396 9000

The Ritz London
• • •
150 Piccadilly, London W1J 9BR

www.theritzlondon.com
enquire@theritzlondon.com
Tel +44 (0) 20 7493 8181

The Soho Hotel
• • •
4 Richmond Mews, London W1D 3DH

www.sohohotel.com
soho@firmdale.com
Tel +44 (0) 20 7559 3000

The Zetter Townhouse
• • •
49-50 St John's Square, London EC1V 4JJ

www.thezettertownhouse.com
info@thezetter.com
Tel +44 (0) 20 7324 4444

York & Albany
• • •
127-129 Parkway, London NW1 7PS

www.gordonramsay.com/yorkandalbany
yorkandalbany@gordonramsay.com
Tel +44 (0) 20 7388 3344

Aster House
• •
3 Sumner Place, London SW7 3EE

www.asterhouse.com
reservations@asterhouse.com
Tel +44 (0) 20 7581 5888

Barclay House London
• •
21 Barclay Road, London SW6 1EJ

www.barclayhouselondon.com
info@barclayhouselondon.com
Tel +44 (0) 20 7384 3390

Church Street Hotel
..
29-33 Camberwell Church Street,
London SE5 8TR

www.churchstreethotel.com
info@churchstreethotel.com
Tel +44 (0) 20 7703 5984

••• expensive
•• mid-range
• inexpensive

CitizenM
..
20 Lavington Street, London SE1 0NZ

www.citizenm.com
supportlba@citizenm.com
Tel +44 (0) 20 3519 1680

Dean Street Townhouse
..
69-71 Dean Street, London W1D 3SE

www.deanstreettownhouse.com
-
Tel +44 (0) 20 7434 1775

Hotel Indigo London - Tower Hill
..
142 Minories, London EC3N 1LS

www.ihg.com
reservations@hitowerhill.com
Tel +44 (0) 20 7423 6310

Hoxton Hotel
..
81 Great Eastern Street, London EC2A 3HU

www.hoxtonhotels.com
-
Tel +44 (0) 20 7550 1000

Mondrian at Sea Container
..
20 Upper Ground, South Bank, London SE1 9PD

www.seacontainerslondon.com
-
Tel +44 (0) 20 3747 1000

No 10 Manchester Street
..
10 Manchester Street, London W1U 4DG

www.tenmanchesterstreethotel.com
ramonac@tenmanchesterstreethotel.com
Tel +44 (0) 20 7317 5900

Threadneedles
..
5 Threadneedle Street, London EC2R 8AY

www.hotelthreadneedles.co.uk
reservations@hotelthreadneedles.co.uk
Tel +44 (0) 20 7657 8080

Clink78
•
78 King's Cross Road, London WC1X 9QG

www.clinkhostels.com
info78@clinkhostels.co.uk
Tel +44 (0) 20 7183 9400

The Green Rooms
•
13-27 Station Road, Wood Green, London N22 6UW

www.greenrooms.london
info@greenrooms.london
Tel +44 (0) 20 8888 5317

Architectural offices

Adjaye Associates
-
Edison House 223-231 Old Marylebone
Road, London NW1 5QT

www.adjaye.com
-
Tel +44 (0) 20 7258 6140

Allford Hall Monaghan Morris
-
Morelands Block C, 5 Old Street, London
EC1V 9HL

www.ahmm.co.uk
-
Tel +44 (0) 20 7251 5261

Allies and Morrison
-
85 Southwark Street, London SE1 0HX

www.alliesandmorrison.com
-
Tel +44 (0) 20 7921 0100

AL_ A
-
14A Brewery Road, London N7 9NH

www.ala.uk.com
-
Tel +44 (0) 20 7243 7670

Arup Associates
-
8 Fitzroy St, Fitzrovia, London W1T 4BJ

www.arupassociates.com
info@arupassociates.com
Tel +44 (0) 20 775 55555

Avery Associates
-
270 Vauxhall Bridge Road . London
SW1V 1BB

www.avery-architects.co.uk
enquiries@avery-architects.co.uk
Tel +44 (0) 20 7233 6262

Farrells
-
7 Hatton Street, London NW8 8PL

www.farrells.com
enquiries@farrells.com
Tel +44 (0) 20 7258 3433

Flanagan Lawrence
-
66 Porchester Road , London W2 6ET

www.flanaganlawrence.com
-
Tel +44 (0) 20 7706 6166

Feilden Clegg Bradley Studios
-
20 Tottenham Street, London W1T 4RG

www.fcbstudios.com
london@fcbstudios.com
Tel +44 (0) 20 7323 5737

Farshid Moussavi Architecture
-
12F, 130 Fenchurch Street, London
EC3M 5DJ

www.farshidmoussavi.com
office@farshidmoussavi.com
Tel +44 (0) 20 7033 6490

Foster + Partners
-
Riverside, 22 Hester Road, London,
SW11 4AN

www.fosterandpartners.com
-
Tel +44 (0) 20 7738 0455

Grimshaw
-
57 Clerkenwell Road, London EC1M 5NG

www.grimshaw-architects.com
-
Tel +44 (0)207 291 4141

Hopkins Architects
-
27 Broadley Terrace, London NW1 6LG

www.hopkins.co.uk
mail@hopkins.co.uk
Tel +44 (0) 20 7724 1751

Jestico + Whiles
-
1 Cobourg Street, London NW1 2HP

www.jesticowhiles.com
info@jesticowhiles.com
Tel +44 (0) 20 7380 0382

John McAslan + Partners
-
7-9 William Road, London NW1 3ER

www.mcaslan.co.uk
-
Tel +44 (0) 20 7313 6000

Make Architects
-
32 Cleveland St, Fitzrovia, London W1T 4JY

www.makearchitects.com
-
Tel +44 (0) 20 7636 5151

Rare Architecture
-
345 Old St, London EC1V

www.r-are.net
info@r-are.net
Tel +44 (0) 20 3239 9332

Rogers Stirk Harbour + Partners
-
The Leadenhall Building, 122 Leadenhall St, London EC3V 4AB

www.rsh-p.com
enquiries@rsh-p.com
Tel +44 (0) 20 7385 1235

Stanton Williams
-
Crystal Wharf, 36 Graham Street, London N1 8GJ

www.stantonwilliams.com
info@stantonwilliams.com
Tel +44 (0) 20 7880 6400

WilkinsonEyre
-
33 Bowling Green Lane, London EC1R 0BJ

www.wilkinsoneyre.com
info@wilkinsoneyre.com
Tel +44 (0) 20 7608 7900

Zaha Hadid Architects
-
9-0 Bowling Green Lane, London EC1R 0bq

www.zaha-hadid.com
-
Tel +44 (0) 20 7253 5147

Index by architect

Index by project

Key to symbols

O••O Less than 10 min walk between the two stations
O Interchange stations
Ⓐ Step-free access from street to train
Ⓐ Step-free access from street to platform
⊕ National Rail
✈ Airport
⛴ Riverboat services
🚌 Victoria Coach Station
🚠 Emirates Air Line cable car

† Services for these stations
are subject to variation.
Please search 'TfL stations'
for full details

Photolithography
LAB di Gallotti Giuseppe Fulvio,
Florence

This volume was printed in August 2020
by Gutenberg Press Limited, Gudja Road,
Tarxien, Malta PLA 19

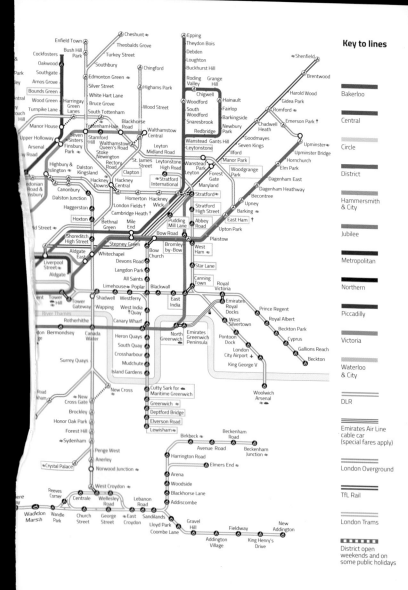

Key to lines

Bakerloo

Central

Circle

District

Hammersmith & City

Jubilee

Metropolitan

Northern

Piccadilly

Victoria

Waterloo & City

DLR

Emirates Air Line cable car (special fares apply)

London Overground

TfL Rail

London Trams

District open weekends and on some public holidays